SEVEN RULES

Ticonius the Donatist

Translated by: D.P. Curtin

Dalcassian
Publishing
Company

Copyright @ 2006 Dalcassian Publishing Company

All rights reserved. No part of this publication may be reproduced, distributed, or transmitted in any form or by any means, including photocopying, recording, or other electronic or mechanical methods, without the prior written permission of the publisher, except in the case of brief quotations embodied in critical reviews and certain other non-commercial uses permitted by copyright law. For permission request, write to Dalcassian Publishing Company at dalcassianpublishing at gmail.com

ISBN: 979-8-8692-0798-2 (Paperback)

Library of Congress Control Number:
Author: Curtin, D.P. (1985-)

Printed by Ingram Content Group, 1 Ingram Blvd, La Vergne, Tennessee

First printing edition 2006.

SEVEN RULES

SEVEN RULES

I thought it necessary, before all that seemed to me, to write a bill of regulations and laws of secrets, as well as to manufacture keys and lights. For there are certain mystical rules which obtain a retreat from the whole law and make the treasures of truth invisible to some. If, as we communicate, the reason for the rules is accepted without envy, all that is closed will be revealed, and the dark things will be made clear, so that anyone walking through the universal forest of prophecy, guided by these rules in a certain way along paths of light, may be protected from error. But these are the rules:

> I. *Of the Lord and his body.*
> II. *On the two-part body of the Lord.*
> III. *Of the promises and read.*
> IV. *Of species and genus.*
> V. *Of the times.*
> VI. *Of the recapitulation.*
> VII. *Of the devil and his body.*

SEVEN RULES

Rule I

Of the Lord and his body.

Scripture speaks of the Lord and his body, that is, the Church (2 Tim. 1:20), reason alone discerns: while it persuades what is appropriate to each one; but the force of truth is so great, it twists it. It is agreed that any other person should teach the duties of different persons to be twofold. Thus, through Isaiah: Here, he says, he bears our sins, and grieves for us, and himself was wounded for our transgressions. God gave him up for our sins, etc. (Isa. 53:4, 6), which is celebrated by every member of the Church to gather in the Lord. And he continues and says about the same thing: And God wants to cleanse him from the plague, and God wants to take away his light from pain, and form him with prudence (Ibid., 10, 11). Does he want to show light to him, whom he delivered for our sins, and to form him with wisdom, since he himself is the light and wisdom of God? and his non-body? Wherefore it is manifest, that it could be seen by reason alone, when he made the transition from the head to the body. Daniel also says that the Lord took a stone cut from the mountain into the body of the kingdoms of the world and crushed it to dust. But his body had effected a mountain, and filled the whole earth. The Lord occupied the whole world by power (Matt. 28:18), and not by the fullness of his body. For they say that the world was filled on that mountain, which it is lawful for a Christian to offer in every place, whereas formerly it was lawful only in Zion. If this is so, it was not necessary to say that the world began from the stone of the mountain effect and growth. For our Lord Christ, before the foundation of the world (John 17:2), had this brightness, and with man he was the Son of God, not little by little, like a stone, but at one time he received all piety in heaven and on earth. And the stone grew into a mountain, and as it grew it covered the whole earth. That which filled the whole earth with his power, was not compared to a stone, not physically. For power is an impalpable thing, but a stone is a palpable body. Nor is the body shown to grow by reason alone, and not the head: the seat is confirmed by Apostolic authority: Having grown, he says, through all things into him who is the head Christ, from whom the whole body is built and connected, through every touch of supply in the measure of each part, he makes the growth of the body, in his edification (Eph. 4, 15, 16). And again: Do not hold on to the head, from which the whole body, constructed and supplied by touch and conjunction, grows into the growth of

God (Col. 2:29). Therefore, it is not the head that is originally the same, but the body grows from the head. Let us return to the purpose. It is written about the Lord's body; He commanded his angels concerning thee to guard thee in all thy ways: they shall bear thee in their hands, lest thy foot stumble upon a stone. You will walk on the asp and the basilisk, and you will trample the lion and the dragon. He called to me, and I will hear him, I am with him in trouble, I will rescue him and glorify him. I will fill him with the length of days, and I will show him my salvation (Ps. 90:11-16). Did God show his savior to those whom he commanded his angels to submit to, and not to his body? Again: Like a bridegroom he put a mitre on me, and like a bride he adorned me with ornaments (Is. 61:10). He said that both sexes of the bridegroom and the bride have one body: but what belongs to the Lord and what belongs to the Church is known by reason. And again: They went out to meet the bridegroom and the bride (Matt. 25:1). He continued, saying, "It is not unless it befits the body: And I will give thee hidden and invisible treasures, and I will open unto thee, that thou mayest know that I am the Lord, who calleth by names, the God of Israel, for the sake of Jacob my son, and Israel my chosen." For because of the testament which he made to the fathers, that they might acknowledge himself, God opened unto the body of Christ invisible treasures, which the eye hath not seen, nor the ear heard, neither have they entered into the heart of man in the body of Christ: but God revealed these things to the church through the Holy Spirit, although this is the grace of God. However, when used in a rational way, sometimes they seem easier. There are others in which this regulation is less clear; by the fact that, whether in the Lord, or in his body, what is rightly said. They can be seen by God's grace and by the grace of God. Thus, the Gospel: In a little while, he says, you will see the Son of Man sitting at the right hand of the power of God and coming with the clouds of heaven (Matt. 26:64). In another place he says: They will not see him coming in the clouds of heaven, except on the last day when all the tribes of the earth are mourning. And then they will see the Son of Man coming in the clouds of heaven (Matt. 24:30). But it is necessary to do both. But first is the coming of the body, that is, according to the Church, coming in the same invisible brightness; then, that is to say, the Lord in the clear glory. For if he had said: You shall see him coming soon, the coming would be understood only as a body. But if you see, you will understand the coming. But now, he says, you will see him coming, because he comes regularly in his body with the brightness of the nativity and similar passions. For if the reborn Christ becomes the members, and the members that make up the body, it is Christ who comes, since the birth is the coming, as it is written: "Illuminate every man that cometh into this world" (John 1:9). And again: Generation goes, and generation goes on (Eccl. 1:4). And again: As you have heard, because the Antichrist is coming (1 John 2:18). Again, about the same body: For if this one who comes preaches another Christ (2 Cor. 11:4). Hence, when the Lord was asked about the signs of his coming, he began to argue about that coming of his, which can be imitated by the enemy's body with signs and wonders: Beware, he says, that no one deceives you (Matt. 24:4). Many will come in my name, that is, in the name of my body. But at the last advent of the Lord, that is, at the consummation of his entire advent, no one would die, as some think. Therefore, let us leave these things more fully to their own order. Nor will it be absurd that we want the whole body to be understood by one, as the Son of man the Church, since the Church, that is, the Sons of God reduced to one body, are called the Son of God, when they are called one man, and also God, just as by the Apostle: Over all that is called God, or that which is worshiped. But that which is worshiped, is the highest God: that he should sit in the temple of God, showing that he himself is God, that is, that he is the Church. Or let him sit in God, to show that he himself is God. But this understanding no less, as we know, Daniel wanted to obscure in the last edict: In the Lord, he says, his place will be glorified (Dan. 11:38): that is, he will be glorified, as the Church in the place of the Church, in the holy place, by the abomination of desolation , in God, that is, in the Church. And the Lord calls the whole people his bride and sister. And the Apostle the Holy Virgin, and against the body, the man of sin. And David says to the whole, Christ, the Church: Showing mercy to his Christ, David, and his seed forever (Ps. 17:51). And the Apostle Paul calls the body of Christ: For as it is one body but has many members; but all the members of one body, although they are many, are one body: so is Christ (1 Cor. 12:12), that is the body of Christ, which is the Church. Again: I rejoice in my passions for you: and I fill up what is lacking in the pressures of Christ (Colossians 1:24), that is, of the Church. For Christ's sufferings lacked nothing: for it is sufficient for the disciple to be like his teacher. In this way, then, we will take the coming of Christ as places. Likewise, in Exodus, we learn that all the sons of God, one son, and all the firstborn of the Egyptians, were the firstborn, thus saying to God: These are the things you will say to Pharaoh: This is what the Lord says: My firstborn son Israel. I said to you: Let my people go, that they may serve me. But you did not want to let him go (Ex. 4:22). Therefore: Behold, I will kill your firstborn son. And David, the vineyard of the Lord, one son, thus said: God of hosts, turn: look down from heaven and see, and visit this vineyard and finish it, which your right hand has planted, and on the son of man, whom thou hast confirmed (Ps. 79:15). And the apostle says the son of God, who is mingled with the son of God: Paul, a servant of Jesus Christ, called an apostle, set apart for the gospel of God, as he had promised through his prophets, in the holy scriptures, about his son, who was made to him, of the seed of David according to the flesh. He who is predestined to be the son of God in weakness, according to the Spirit of sanctification from the resurrection of Jesus Christ our Lord (Rom. 1, 1-4). If he were to say of his son, as from the resurrection of the dead, he would show one son; But now, he says, about his son, from the resurrection of our Lord Jesus Christ from the dead. But he who became the son of God by the resurrection of Christ, shows more openly about his son, because he was made to him, from the seed of David according to the flesh, who is the predestined son of God. Indeed, our Lord is not a predestined son of God, because he is God, and is co-equal with the Father, who from whom he was created, that is. But he to whom, according to Luke, during baptism says: You are my son, today I have begotten you (Ps. 2:7). He who was of the seed of David, was mixed with the principal Spirit, and became himself the son of God, from the resurrection of our Lord Jesus Christ: that is, when the seed of David rose to Christ: not he, of whom David himself said: Thus, saith the Lord to my Lord (Ps. 90:1). And so, they became two, one flesh, the Word was made flesh (John 1:14), and flesh God: for we were not born of blood, but of God. The apostle says: They shall be two in one flesh. This sacrament is great: but I say, in Christ and in the Church (Eph. 5:31, 32). For God promised Abraham one seed; so that no matter how many Christs are mixed together, they may be united in Christ, as the apostle says: You are all one in Christ Jesus. But if you are one in Christ Jesus, then you are the seed of Abraham, and according to the promise you will inherit (Gal. 3:28, 29). Whenever one is mixed with the other by will, they are one. As the Lord says: I and the Father are one (John 10:3). But whenever they are both corporeally mixed, and the two are solidified into one flesh: they are one body. And so, the Son of God is in his head; and God in his body, is the son of man, who comes every day at birth, and grows into the holy temple of God. For the temple is divided into two parts. Whose altar, though it be built with great stones, is destroyed: and in it shall not be left one stone upon another.

Rule II

Of the divided body of the Lord.

The rule of the two-parted body of the Lord would be much more necessary for us to understand so much more carefully, and the entire Scriptures must be kept before our eyes. For just as, as was said above, it seems rational from the head to the body: thus, from part of the body to part, from right to left, or from left to right, the return to the aforesaid head is clear. For while he says to one body: I will open invisible treasures for you, so that you may know that I am God, and I will receive you (Is. 45:3): and he added: But you did not know me, because I am God, and there is no other God besides me. And you did not know me (Ibid. 4:5). Although one body is addressed, it meets in one mind, I will open invisible treasures to you, so that you may know that I am God, because of my son Jacob: And you did not know me? In the same: and Jacob did not receive what God promised. It does not agree with the mind: But you knew the menon, and you did not know me. But you did not know that it is said to him, who may have been called to this, that he might know, and that he is visibly of the same body, and indeed approaches the lips of God; yet let him be separated from the heart. He said to him, "But you did not know me." Again: I will lead the blind in a way which they have not known, and in paths which they have not known, they will tread and I will make darkness for them light, and crookedness for the straight. These words I will do, and I will not forsake them. But he himself turned back (Is. 42:16, 17). Have those whom He said I will not leave turned back, and not a part of them? Again, the Lord says to Jacob: Fear not, for I am with you. I will bring your seed from the East and gather you from the West. I will say to the North, give it; and Africa, do not forbid. I will bring my sons from a distant land, and I will take my daughters to the earth, and all in whom my name is called. For in my glory, I prepared him and the child, and produced blind people, and their eyes are likewise blind, and they have deaf ears (Is. 43:5, 8). Are those whom he prepared for his glory, the same blind and deaf? Again: Your fathers first; They admitted the deeds of the princes to me, and they defiled my holy things to the princes, and I gave Jacob to perish, and Israel uncursed (Ibid. 25). Now listen to me, my son Jacob, and Israel whom I have chosen (Is. 44:1). He pointed out to him that he had given Jacob to perish, and Israel to a curse, which he had not chosen. Again: I made you my child, you are mine, Israel, do not forget me. For behold, I have blotted out your sins like a cloud, and like a cloud. Turn to me, and I will redeem you (Ibid. 21). Is he whose sins he has blotted out, to whom he says, 'You are mine': And lest he should forget himself, he mentions the same thing and says, 'turn to me,' or are the sins of anyone before he is converted, be blotted out? Again: I know that when you are rejected, you will be rejected: for your name's sake, I will show you my dignity, and I will bring you my excellencies (Is. 48:8, 9). Does he show his dignity to the reprobate, and bring forth his excellent things to him? Again: Not an elder, not an Angel: but he considered them because he loved them and spared them. He himself redeemed them, and assumed them, and exalted them all the ages. But they were disobedient and provoked the Holy Spirit (Is. 63:9-10). Who has exalted all the days of the world, at what time were they disobedient, or did they provoke the Holy Spirit? the rich city, the tabernacles that will not be moved, nor will the poles of your tent be moved for eternity, and its ropes will not be broken (Is. 33:20). and he will not remove the sign until he is delivered into destruction (Ibid. 23). Again, he briefly shows the two-parted body of Christ: He will take the dark color (Song 1:4). For it is far from the case that the Church, which has no spot or wrinkle (Eph. 5:27), which the Lord has cleansed with His blood, has been darkened in some part, except on the left side, through which the name of God was blasphemed among the nations. Otherwise, it is all beautiful, as he says. You are all beautiful, my neighbor: and there is no reproach in you (Song 4:7). In fact, he says from what because he caused the dark and beautiful: like cedar tents, and Solomon's skins. For Kedar is the son of Ishmael. Finally, in another place, with this Cedar, that is, with the servant from Abraham, the Church closed its long residence, saying: Alas for me! for my pilgrimage has been far: I have dwelt with cedar tents, my soul has traveled much When I made peace with those who hated me, I was peaceful: when I spoke to them, they fought me for nothing (Ps. 119:5-7). But I cannot say that the Tabernacle of Cedar is apart from the Church. For he himself says: Solomon's tabernacle will stand. Wherefore I am brown, he says, and beautiful. For the church is not brown among those who are outside. In this mystery the Lord in the Apocalypse says seven angels, that is, the seven-fold church, now the guardians of the holy and precepts: now the same and shows those guilty of many crimes and those worthy of penance. whom the Lord divides into two parts (Luke 19:21). I say: will he divide everything, or will he find? Finally, not the whole, but a part of it will be placed with the hypocrites (Matt. 24:51). In one he shows his body. And this body is to be accepted by all the scriptures, where God says, for the merit of Israel, that he shall perish, and curse his inheritance. For the apostle argues copiously, especially to the Romans, that whatever has been said about the whole body should be accepted. To Israel, he says, "All day I stretched out my hands against the people who contradicted me" (Rom. 10:21). And in order to show what was said on the other hand: I say, he says, Has God rejected his people? He is away. For I too am an Israelite of the seed of Abraham, of the tribe of Benjamin. God did not reject his common people, which he foresaw (Rom. 11:1, 2). And after he taught how this expression was to be understood; In the same kind of expression, he shows that both good and evil are one body, saying: According to the Gospel, indeed, enemies for your sakes: but according to the election, beloved for the sake of the fathers (Ib. 28). Thus, the Lord testifies in all the Scriptures that one body of Abraham's seed grows and flourishes and perishes in all nations.

Rule III

Of the promises and the Law.

Paul explains to Rom. and to Gal., and Isaiah. c. 48. It is a divine authority that no one could ever be justified by the works of the law. It is most certain by the same authority that there was no lack of those who broke the law and were justified. the world to God. Because all flesh is not justified by the law in his sight. For by the law, you are acknowledged to have sinned (Rom. 3:19, 20). Again: Your sin will not rule. For you are not under the law (Rom. 6:4). We believe in Christ: that he may be justified by faith, and not by the works of the law (Gal. 2:16). Again: For if the law had been given which could give life, it would have been justice in every way by the law. be given to those who believe (Gal. 3:21, 22). wanting to put a yoke on the neck of the learners, which neither our fathers nor we were able to bear (Acts 15:10). And on the contrary, the same Apostle says: Justice, which is from the law, is preserved without complaint (Philipp. 3:6). What if the authority of such an Apostle was lacking: what could be said against the testimony of the Lord who said: Behold! Truly an Israelite in which there is no deceit (John 1:47). What if the Lord had not designed to bear this testimony: who would be so blasphemous, who would be so puffed up with swelling stupor, that Moses and the Prophets, even the saints, did not do justice, or that they were not justified? When the Scripture says about Zechariah and his answer: They were both righteous in the sight of God, walking in all the commandments and justifications of God without complaint (Luke 1:6). And the Lord did not come to call the righteous, but sinners (Matt. 9:13). which is given to this: But the law entered in, that sin might multiply (Rom. 5:20). But we should know that we should hold: that the seed of Abraham was never completely intercepted, from Isaac until today. but it is from the promise. For the second seed is carnal, which is from the law from Mount Sinai, which is Hagar begetting in slavery. He indeed, of whom the handmaid was born carnally. And the apostle says that there is no seed of Abraham except that which is of faith: You know then that those who are of faith are the children of Abraham (Gal. 3:7)? And again: And you, brothers according to Isaac, are children of the promise (Gal. 4:28). The seed of Abraham, then, is not of the law, but of the promise, which continually passes from Isaac. For the law and faith are different. Because the law is not of faith, but of works. For the promise is not of the law to Abraham, or to his seed, that he should be an heir of the world, but by the righteousness of faith. Abraham can be destroyed, he remained continually from his birth. Nor, given the law, was it hindered, so that Abraham's sons could not be pledged according to the promise. For the apostle says that after four hundred and thirty years the law given did not exist, nor did it destroy the promise: For if from the law, then not from promise. And to Abraham, God gave a promise (Ibid., 18). And in another place: Is the law therefore contrary to God's promises? Just as the law was never present to faith, faith did not destroy the law. As it is written: We destroy the law through faith? But out of faith by a promise. Now we must inquire how those who were denied the works of the law, could be justified, were placed in the law, and those who worked the law were justified. We must also inquire why, after the promise of faith, which could in no way be destroyed, the law was given, which is not of faith: By whose works no one would be justified, because, as many as are by the works of the law, they are under the curse. For it is written: Cursed is he who does not continue in all things that are written in the book of the law, that he may do them (Gal. 3:10). had asserted in every way that the sons of God had always been by faith, not by the law of works, he answered him in the person of another, saying: What then is the law of works (Rom. 3:27)? begetting the sons of Abraham, and were they to be nourished by faith? For the just lives by faith (Rom. 1:17; Gal. Heb. 10, 30). For before he asked himself: What then is the law of works? He had already said, let those who could not be justified by faith live, in this way: For by the law no one is justified with God, but the just live by faith (Gal. 3:11). Placed to live, unless he had done the works of the law, and all the works: otherwise, he would have been cursed. For it is necessary for the passions of sins, which are by the law, to work in the members of him who is in the law. For this reason, they were given: that sin might abound (Rom. 5:20), because the power of sin is the law. works good but does not will evil: for he consents to the law, according to the inner man. But in another way, he is attacked by the law of the members, he is dragged and taken captive, and could never be freed, except by grace through faith alone. On the other hand, it is of great faith to have searched and seen. It is, therefore, sacrilege, and feeling ill of God, that with no law a man can be made human, and he sees that he is ready to take revenge; he did not understand that there was any remedy for life: nor could it have been, that the good God, who knew that the law could not be done, had not left another approach to life: and against men whom he had made to life, he had closed the ways of life on every side. This faith did not take, did not admit, and was forced

SEVEN RULES

by the power of sin: God gave clarity. Knowing that the Lord is good and just, and that he did not close the bowels of his compassion against the work of his hands: he understood that he had to live again, and he saw the remedy of doing the law. He did not expose himself, as that might have been the case, but truly and decidedly said: Thou shalt not covet; because he leaves it to be discovered. For if he commanded that the result should be demanded from himself, he would have destroyed the law and faith. For what would he give to the law, if he promised the law in all things done? lovers of life, let them see life by faith, and the righteous, let them live by faith, who believe that the work of the law can be done not by their own power, but by the gift of God. of death: except by the help and mercy of God, what does faith find? It is not subject to the dear law of God; for he cannot. But those who are incarnate cannot please God. But you are not in the flesh, but in the spirit; indeed, the Spirit of God is in you. But if anyone does not have the Spirit of Christ, he is not his (Rom. 8:7, 9). He shows that the Spirit of God and Christ are the same. The Spirit of God and Christ is one; and the holy prophets, because they had the Spirit of God, they had the Spirit of Christ. If they had the Spirit of God, they were not in the flesh, and did the law: for the flesh is enmity with God, and is not subject to his law. ; which being mortified, he could make the spiritual law, freed from the law, because it was not laid down by the righteous. And again: If you walk by the Spirit of God, you are not under the law (Gal. 5:18). They were under the law. For as long as anyone is in the flesh, that is, does not have the Spirit of God, he is dominated by the law. But if he surrenders himself to grace, he dies to the law, and the spirit makes the law in him, dead flesh, which cannot be subject to the law of God. this is also carried on now, for it is not because we are not under the law that the prohibition of concupiscence has ceased, nor has it been increased; but we come to the revealed grace through faith, taught by the Lord, to demand the work of the law out of his mercy, and to say: Thy will be done: And, deliver us from evil (Matthew 6:10, 13). They saw that the minister of the law was ready to be stabbed with a sword. as if faith could not be expressed without the law, to seek the grace of God, because it had no power to sin. We suffered the custody of a prison, threatened with death by the law, and surrounded on all sides by an insurmountable wall, whose perimeter was the only door of grace. The guardian of this door, faith, presided: so that no one could escape from that prison, unless he opened it to the faithful; and whoever did not knock at this door would die within the walls of the law. is the end of the law, by which all lived who sought the faith of God's grace. Before faith came, we were kept under the law, we were shut up in faith, which was to be revealed. Therefore, the law was our teacher in Christ (Gal. 3:24): that we might be justified by faith. The law, I say, faith was demonstrative. but after the promise of Abraham's sons, when they were multiplied according to the flesh, the seed of Abraham should also be multiplied, which is not unfaithful. This multiplication cannot take place without the multiplication of the auxiliary laws, and the multitude be brought into faith not yet revealed, as has already been said, or by necessity. Providence therefore God, by increasing the sanctity and guiding the seed of Abraham, so that by the severity and fear of the law, many were compelled to faith, and the seed was supported until the revelation of faith: But the law entered in, that sin might multiply. Where, he says, sin multiplied, grace abounded. He did not say, born, but abounded. For from the beginning troubles and dominion were given to those fleeing from the law. near and who is far (Is. 57, 19; Ephesians 2:17), that is, to the sinners of Israel and the Gentiles. For righteous Israel was called by faith to the same faith. For the same spirit, the same faith, the same grace was always given through Christ, which did not differ from those who were to come. For otherwise there was never a seed of Abraham. If anyone was justified apart from faith, he was not a son of Abraham. For he cannot be called a son of Abraham, if he was justified by the law, and not like Abraham, by faith. For the image of grace and the spirit passed into the same church, the Apostle teaches, saying: But we all, beholding the revealed glory of God, are changed into the same image, from brightness to brightness (II Cor. 3, 18). They could be excluded by law, that is, expressed, produced, made possible. Whence, it is clear that it was from faith. but by the law of faith (Rom. 3:27, 28). For what does the Scripture say? Abraham believed God, and it was counted to him as righteousness (Rom. 4:3). it was from works, it has glory, but not to God. Indeed, it is impossible, without the grace of God, to have any glory. In fact, there is only one glory, and it has always been of one kind. But in faith, God makes our adversary weak. Let him who glories glory in the Lord (1 Cor. 1:31). For if what we overcome is not ours: it is not from works, but from faith. We have nothing that we have not received. If we are, we are from God: so that the greatness of the power is God's, and none of us. All our work is faith. God works in us as much as it has been. but that man's continence is a gift of God: When I knew, he said, because I cannot be continuous in any other way, unless God gave it. it is to be believed, not by their works, but by the grace of God, that all who are justified have chosen to fulfill the work of the law by God, by which they may be glorified.

And the apostle says: That all flesh may not be glorified in the sight of God (1 Cor. 1, 29). they knew: the righteous, that they are not their own work, but God's work. Useless things, he says, and God cast away those things which are not: that those things which are, may be emptied, that all flesh may not glory in the sight of God. wisdom from God, and righteousness, and sanctity, and redemption have become for you: that according to what is written: Let him be glorified, let him glory in the Lord (Ibid., 28-30). And again: By grace you have been saved through faith, and this not of yourselves (Eph. 2:8). It is a gift of God, not of works, lest any man should glory for we are his likeness, created in Christ. Thus, no flesh shall be chosen at any time, that is, it may be justified by works, that every righteous man may have glory from God. another thing, that no one should glory in the sight of God: for God works in this way, so that it may be that he also forgives: Let no one be separated from the world by dirt, nor if his life be for one day (Job 14:4). And David says: You shall not enter into judgment with your servant, since all living will not be justified by your disregard (Ps. 142:2). For who will boast that he has a chaste heart? Or who will boast that he is clean? There was little of a chaste heart, that is, of thoughts, unless he was clean of sin. is: Who crowns you with compassion and mercy (Ps. 104:4). And the mother of martyrs says to her son: That I may receive you with those compassions of your brothers (II Mac.7:29). they desire to serve God, but not in the law. Which if he justified, all would be righteous by the merit of one, because it seems that he demands observance of all; glory, as by the spirit of God, that is, from the same to the same? Such is the extension, because after Christ faith was given: what kind, because the Holy Spirit, when all the prophets and the righteous always lived by the same spirit. For they could not live otherwise than by the spirit of faith. They were by the law, they were killed. For the letter kills, but the spirit gives life (2 Cor. 3:6). And yet the Lord says of the same Spirit: "Except I go away, he will not come" (John 16:7), when he already gave the same spirit to the apostles. (2 Cor. 4, 13). He said that he had the same spirit of faith, who said: I believed because of what I spoke (Ps. 115:1): and he confirmed this, saying: And we believe; and that is why we speak. Saying: And we, he shows that they also believed in the same spirit of faith. Whence it is clear that the righteous always had these things, not from the law, but by the spirit of faith. Whatever comes through the Lord is the fullness, of which he was a part as well. Just as the little one, who since there is nothing less than a man, yet he is not a man, and through the growth of not new members, but of the same members, the fullness of the body came to him, that he might be perfect, yet the same as if he had been a child. Indeed, the Holy Spirit was not in all before the passion of the Lord; but in them they believed that he was present, that they might be sealed and perfected by the conqueror himself, who was completing everything. Nor, since it is different, can it be mixed. The non-condition weakens the promise; but we are forced to speak to ourselves those things which we cannot hear without the fire of pain. For some say, who do not know the firmness of promises, and the transgression of what is from the law: that the God of Abraham had indeed promised all nations (but with the exception of free will, if they kept the law. It is useful to reveal the safety of some of the righteous; but when there is talk of God Almighty, we must moderate what we say, lest we be considered to be silent, and be heard from our own mouth, even if it be another's. not futures. It is the other of the two: if futures, the question is finished; if not the future, a faithful God would not promise. Or if this is the law of God, then to give the promise, if they were willing to promise: surely, he would say, lest his servant and believer, because what he promised, he is able to do, should make fun of Abraham. But that promise is that which incurs no condition. Neither the promise is firm, nor the faith complete. For what will remain stable in the promise of God, or in the faith of Abraham, if that which was promised and believed depended on the discretion of those who promised? Therefore, God also promised a stranger, and Abraham believed recklessly. So what even the promise itself was made due afterwards, saying to God: Let all the nations of the earth be blessed in thee, because thou hast heard my voice, and hast not spared thy beloved son for my sake (Gen. 22:18)? slanders of discretion; Even after the death of Abraham, God confirms himself as a debtor, and for his sake, he would do what he promised to each of his sons, saying: I will be with you and bless you. yours as the stars of heaven, and I will give to you and to your seed all the nations of the earth, because your father Abraham heard my voice (Gen. 26:3-5). Behold, Abraham's debt was confirmed. ; yet the nations would not believe. What will Abraham do, to whom he owes? How will he accept the debt of his faith and temptation, which he was sure he owed to God? To whom it was said: I will give what I promised, and I will repay what I swore (Ibid., 4): if the nations willed, he would not believe, but if there is a need for a condition, it must be with the worker, not with a wage. For the worker can be willing to accept or not, not to be paid or not to be paid. For all the nations were given to Abraham without reward of faith, as God says: Your reward is great (Gen. 15:1). For he promised not if they were to come, and not because they were to come. Because it pleased God not because of the faith of Abraham, that all nations should be saved: which he possessed not only before the faith of Abraham, but before the constitution of the world. from whom he was, whose future he had determined. Abraham therefore did not deserve it, that they should be those who were to come, whom God had chosen, and had foreseen that they would be conformed to the image of his son. He will become a great and numerous nation and all the nations of the earth will be blessed in him (Gen. 26:16). Whatever he spoke to him. And we also find conditions, such as: If you will hear me and be willing. Where is the foreknowledge of God, where is the firmness of the promise in such conditions? (Rom. 4:16). The law, he says, works wrath; where also there is no law, nor transgression (Ibid., 15). It is by faith that according to grace the promise is firm to every seed. Rightly, that the promise was firm. Moreover, it is not firm by condition. It is said. Let God say to them: Yes, you will hear those whom He knew would hear, whom He knew before He made, that they would persevere in the image of God, whom He had promised. There is no condition given, that is the law, except to the ungodly and sinners: that they may either flee to grace, or to the just let them be punished if they have done something invalid. For what is the law to the righteous, to whom the law is not laid, who in propriety make the law without the law to God, who serve, what to the image and likeness of God and Christ, who live by will, are good? For he who is under the law, for fear of death, he is not like that, merciful, I do not esteem God. The law displeases him: but he fears vengeance and cannot complete it which he supposes to be done not by desire, but by necessity. It must be surrendered to one's own will; that the will may surely receive the reward, because the soul has not mingled with the will of God. The separation is what God has willed. He is not united to God, who would not be subject to a similar punishment, evil would follow. it is necessary, convinced and conquered, he who is carnal under the power of sin, not having the Spirit of God. But he who loves good, is the image of God, lives by the faith of the Lord, and is an heir, no longer the son of a virgin (Gal. 4, 30, 31), who received the law inwardly ; but free, according to Isaac, who did not receive the spirit of slavery in fear, but the adoption of children, crying Abba father (Rom. 8:15). He who loves God does not fear servilely. It is one thing to be afraid of the law, another for the reverence of the tremendous majesty of God. Such are they like unto their father in heaven: remember that the learned love good, hate evil. Indeed, he can hear: will it come to him whom God has not yet foreseen that he will hear? But for another reason, not because they cannot disobey: but that they may always be anxious for their salvation, etc. for their own exit. For not everyone is sure that he is among the number of the forerunners, saying to the Apostle: Lest I myself be reprobate (1 Cor. 9:27). That law is the worker of wrath, but the exercise of faith, whereby those who labor constantly seek God's grace, so that what God has foreseen in them may be accomplished, and they may be destined to life of their own free will. Otherwise, it is impossible not to listen to him whom God foresaw, promised, swore to hear. Part of the law is appropriate, although it is given to one body, the Lord declares in the Gospel, saying to the apostles: If you know these things, blessed are you if you do them. For if he had said: I do not speak of all of you; or, I say not of all, he would not show one body. Now I do not say of all: he shows because and if not of all, yet he said of them. common, one body is praised or rebuked. Just as in Exodus, when a certain man went out on the Sabbath to gather manna, God said to Moses: How long will you not listen to my law (Ex. 16:26)? when Moses always listened. Does it seem contrary to the promise? It is written in Isaiah: If you had listened to me, Israel, your number would have been like the sand of the sea (Is. 48:18). Behold, Israel is reprimanded because by his sin he was not made like the sand of the sea. And where is the firmness of the promises? But this happens because we want to understand before we believe and submit faith to reason. But if we believe that it will be done in every way as God has sworn, faith will give reason. How treacherous we are to look for reason, and we understand that the firmness of promises is greater than what we think is weakness. For this was said: If Israel had heard, it is a commemoration of the justice of God, and a confirmation of the promises, by the dispoforion of God some are made to die, and some to life. because he foresaw those who would hear. For before the Lord Christ, when this was said, the seed of Abraham was never like the sand of the sea? This is easy to prove. First, because in Christ he promised this multitude: not in seeds as in many, but as in one, and your seed, which is Christ (Gal. 3:16). Then, because he promised all the nations, that could not be done before Christ. For not, because all are from Abraham, all the children of Abraham; even Israel, all Israel. Just as the Apostle, when he wished to be Anathema for Israel (Rom. 9:3), whose sons were adopted and testaments, he shows that they were not the sons of Abraham, but that he grieved because of the feeling of carnal necessity, because they were not of his own number. the promise of God had fallen out, saying: Yet the word of God has not fallen out, for not all who are of Israel are Israel, nor because they are the seed of Abraham, are they all children: but in Isaac shall be called your seed:

that is, not those who are children of the flesh, these are the children of God: but the children of the promise are appointed as seed (Ibid., 6-8). Therefore, there was no Abraham in the ancient population: except for those who, according to Isaac, were children of faith and of the promise. The remnants will be delivered, that is, a little (Is. 10:12; Hos. 1:10). so that it would be Sodom. Again, when he asserted that he had never left his inheritance to God: but as at the coming of the Lord, part of Israel was saved: so, it had always been (Rom. 11:4). So now the remnants are saved according to the election, saying: If now in this time: it shows what happened in Israel before, so that the remnant, that is, a little saved. But if neither faith nor reason convinces the faith, who had been promised, had said: If you had heard me, Israel; your number would be like the sand of the sea (Is. 48:18). And Jacob, as soon as he was born, was given: the same free will was later rejected. I was repaid (Hos. 12:2): because in the womb he supplanted his brother, and in his labors he grew strong toward God, and he grew strong with the angel (Gen. 25:23; Rom. 9:10). But if it is true, in Jacob the beloved is not the same who in his labors has grown up to God and the supplanter, but two in one body. For he is a figure of the double seed of Abraham, that is, of two peoples struggling in one womb of the mother of the Church. And Jacob and Esau are in one body, from one seed. and the brother's substitute is expressed. Thus, in two the quantity is expressed, not the quality of the separation. Moreover, both who are separated in the one future, before they are divided, are shown. Unless this is a mystical expression, briefly showing two in one body: is it not contrary to reason, that he received a blessing in the treacherous neighbor, the Scripture saying: He who did not swear to his neighbor in treachery; will he receive a blessing from the Lord (Ps. 23:4)? But Jacob, that is, the Church, never comes to the blessing, not accompanied by idols, that is, false brothers. But no, because innocence and deceit come together to the blessing, they are blessed together: let him take (Matt. 19:12), and one seed for the quality of the earth came forth. But it is not the opposite, that he seems to have supplanted his evil brother, because he did not say: He supplanted Esau inwardly, but his brother Jacob, took both: for that reason, that the bad part pretends to be Jacob, and without doubt, with one name: but the good part, cannot pretend to be Esau. nor Esau all evil, but from both. From Abraham the two-parted seed was thus shown. One was born from a handmaid in a figure (Gal. 4:22): so that the future servants from Abraham might also be shown, and he withdrew with his mother. with the seed of another, which is free, which is from Israel, who received the law on Mount

Sinai, which is Hagar procreating in slavery. There, according to Isaac, many children of the promise, that is, holy and faithful, were procreated to the same people. , in one people all the latter comes. From there both testaments, Hagar and Isaac; Just as then, under the profession of the Old Testament, the new was hidden, that is, grace, according to which Isaac would beget children of the promise out of free will, which was revealed in Christ: so also now that the new has been obtained, there is no lack of servitude to the children of Hagar, which will be revealed in Christ. The Apostle confirms that now also to be done among the brethren, what was done among them at that time, saying: But you, brethren according to Isaac, are the children of the promise. But what does the Scripture say? Let the slave girl cast out her son: for the son of the slave woman will not be bound to the son of the free woman (Ibid., 30). so even now, it is not in vain. He was persecuted until the Apostles were interpreted. For the Scripture says: Ishmael was playing with Isaac (Gen. 21:9). As, therefore, he said, the persecutor is degenerate in playing: so also those who, as if by common interest, that is, the discipline of the law, separate the children of God from Christ, and their mother Hagar, serve as children. For there is no other reason why the children of the devil creep in to spy out our freedom, and pretend to be brothers, and in our paradise to play as if they were the children of God: than to glory in the subdued freedom of the children of God, who will bear judgment, whatever they may be, who persecuted all the saints, who killed the prophets , who always resisted the Holy Spirit; the enemies of the cross of Christ, denying Christ in the flesh, while they were members of him, the body of sin, the children of extermination, the ministry of evildoers, who come according to the operation of Satan in all power, signs and wonders, spiritual iniquity in the heavenly places: whom the Lord Christ, whom they persecute in the flesh, will kill in his spirit, and he will destroy it by the manifestation of his coming. For it is time that these ministrations, if they should be properly called, are imminent departure, which is the revelation of man's sin, when Lot left Sodom.

Rule IV

On species and species.

The light quoted in Ezekiel, chapter 27 and 32 and 36 and 37, Isaiah 13 and 24, Jeremiah 25. We are talking about species and species, not according to the rhetorical power of human wisdom, which he could more than anyone else, he did not speak, lest he would have made the cross of Christ empty, if but we speak according to the mysteries of heavenly wisdom, by the mastery of the Holy Spirit. the body, as in Solomon. But this is no less hidden than the rest, which are hidden not only by the form of the word, but also by many forms of narration. We must work out that the spirit multiplies the entry of the reading, and the subtle speech, which in order to hinder the intellect, the species, or the genus, inserts a species: the species does not exist, it can be easily seen. he sets forth words which agree both internally and externally, until he gradually exceeds the mode of the species, and the transition becomes clear, when those which began with the species only agree into the genus, and in the same way he leaves the genus, returning to the species. , and it evidently returns to a variety of a similar order: either from aspect to genus, or from genus to species, it ends the narrative, which was the grace of God. Thus, the Lord speaks through Ezekiel, and of the kings who had been captured and dispersed from Jerusalem, he joins the arrival of the nations, and expresses the world in the land which our fathers possessed. For the seven nations promised to Abraham are the figure of all nations. The word of the Lord came to me, saying: Son of man, the house of Israel dwelled in the earth, and defiled it in their way, and in the idols of their sins: according to the uncleanness of the menses, their way was made before my face. And I poured out my wrath upon them and scattered them among the nations. which they have entered, and have profaned my holy name there: while they say, these are the Lord's people, and they have gone out of your land; : Thus saith the Lord: I will not do it unto you, O house of Israel: but because of the holy name which you have polluted among the nations, in the midst of which you have entered. and the nations shall know that I am the Lord, who will be sanctified in you before the eyes of the eyes; , and I will cleanse you, and I will give you a new heart, and I will put a new spirit in you, and I will take away the heart of stone from your flesh: and I will give you flesh, and I will put my spirit in you, and I will make you walk in my righteousness, and keep my judgments, and work. And you shall dwell in the land which I gave to your fathers. And you shall be my people, and I will be your God, and I shall cleanse you from all your filthiness (Ez. 36:17, 28). and I will multiply it: and I will not give you famine, and I will multiply the fruit of the tree, and that which grows in the field: that you may no longer receive reproaches, among the nations, and remember your wicked ways, your thoughts that are not good, and that you may not be hated before their face in your iniquities, and for their abominations. I do it not for your sake, says the Lord. It is known to you, be confused and turn back from your ways, house of Israel. This is what the Lord says: In the day when I will cleanse you from all your iniquities, and make the cities intoxicated, in the image of the land of Judah, that which had been laid waste by wars, will be worshiped, because it was exterminated under the eyes of all who passed by. Because I am the Lord. is: He will come from Zion who will deliver and remove ungodliness from Jacob (Rom. 11:25, 26). The same kind of expression returns to the species, saying: According to the Gospel, indeed, the enemies are because of you. Also in Ezekiel, it begins with the species, which should agree in the genus, and ends in a single class, showing that the land is the possession of the fathers of the world. And they shall no longer be divided into two nations, nor shall they be divided into two kingdoms: lest they be still defiled by their hypocrisy (Ez. 37:21, 23). It passes openly into the genus: And my servant David will be a prince in their midst, the one shepherd of all who will walk in my precepts, and keep my judgments, and do them, and dwell in their land, which I have given to my servant Jacob, where their fathers dwelt, and they shall dwell therein, and David my servant, their prince forever, and I will arrange for them a covenant of peace, and it shall be an everlasting covenant with them. , and I will be their God: and they will be my people. And the nations will know that I am the Lord who sanctifies them, while they are holy in their midst, says the Lord (Ibid., 24, 28). Also, there I went out of the dispersion of Israel, the arrival of the nations is planted. that they were a desert people, in which the Church now is, is made manifest: and that even though the same people, together with the people of God from the nations, are recalled from the land of Israel, they are not in the land. it shall be as you say. We shall be like the nations, and like the tribes of the earth, that we may serve wood and stone. As I live, says the Lord, I will rule over you only in a strong hand and a high arm, and I will reign over you in the outpouring of wrath, and I will raise you up from the peoples and take you from the countries , in which you were scattered with a strong hand and a high arm, and anger poured out, and I will bring you into the wilderness of the peoples, and I will argue with you face to face: as I argued with your fathers in the wilderness of the land of Egypt, so will I judge you, says the Lord, and bring you under my rod , and I will bring you in number, and I will choose the wicked from among you and deserters: for I will bring them up from their transmigration, and they will not enter the whole of Israel, and you will know that the Lord is selfish (Ez. 20:31, 38). God promises the abundance of the mountains of Israel, and the multiplication of the peoples to infinity. Behold, I have spoken in my jealousy, and in my anger, because of the reproach of the nations you have borne. Behold, I will lift up my hand upon the nations which are round about you. is near to come. For behold, I am upon you, and I will plant and sow: and I will multiply upon you the house of Israel to the end, and cities shall be inhabited, and those that were desolate shall be built (Ez. 36:5, 10). Also there, as in the last resurrection, the first is signified: He spoke, he said, to me, saying: Son of man, these bones are the whole house of Israel. They say: Our bones have become dry, our hope has died, we have expired. Thus, saith the Lord: Behold, I will open your graves, and bring you up from your graves, and bring you into the land of Israel, and you shall know that I am the Lord, I will open your graves, and bring up my people from the graves, and I will put my spirit into you, and you shall live. I will set you upon your earth, and you shall know that I am the Lord (Ez. 37, 11, 14). Shall we clearly know the Lord when we rise again, and not now, when we rise through baptism? Or the dead will be able to say: Our bones are dried up, he that heareth my voice, and believeth in him that sent me, hath eternal life, and shall not come into judgment, but shall pass from death unto life. For just as the Father has life in himself, so he gave the Son to have life in himself. all who are in the tombs will hear the voice of the Son of God, and those who have done good will come out to the resurrection of life: but those who have done evil to the resurrection of judgment (Ibid., 28, 29). First, he said, the dead who hear will live. Second, all who are in the tombs will come out. Likewise, as the whole body is signified in one man, God promises David in the book of Kings, saying of Solomon: I will raise up his kingdom: he will build my house (2 Kings 7:15), saying: And I will direct his throne to eternity. Likewise, and inwardly: I will be his father, and he will be my son, but I will not take my mercy away from him, as I have removed from those whom I have removed from my sight, and we will become faithful to him. , and his throne will be established and established for eternity (Ibid., 13, 16). Since it seems in excess to promise the throne of Christ for eternity, he promises the throne of the Son of Man, and thus the Body of Christ, that is, of the Church. For it was not because of David that God promised that Christ would reign: to whom before the foundation of the world he promised this glory. And through Isaiah, God says to Christ thus: This will be great for you: that you may call my son, and turn the dispersion of Jacob to the statues, and Israel. Behold, I have set you as a testament of the race, as a light of the nations, that you may be saved forever to the end of the earth (Is. 49:6). What is greater that my child should be called the Son of God, and that Israel should convert the dispersion, or that Israel itself and the heavens and the earth, and all that is in them visible and invisible? He is of the seed of God. , or was he rejected after idolatry? If we say with God: we will guarantee impunity to the worshipers of idols. For the Scripture does not say that Solomon repented, or that he received wisdom. Kings: I will tear your kingdom from your hand, and I will give it to your servant. Truly, I will not do this in your days, for the sake of David, your father. I will take it from the hand of your son. , and for the sake of Jerusalem, the city which I have chosen, (3 Kings 11:11, 14). For what is the benefit of David, if his son succeeded him in the kingdom of the earth, and he is to perish from heaven? for David's sake, as he had said: I will lay his sins on the rod of men: but I will not take away my mercy from him (2 Kings 7:14). That if he is neither reprobate, nor idol worshipers inherit the kingdom of God: it is manifest that he has rejected the figure of the two-part church, Solomon, whose breadth of heart and wisdom are like the sand of the sea, and idolatry is terrible. For I have shown the future of Solomon always in his son, that is, in his posterity: in the days of Solomon's posthumous God does not take away the kingdom, according to the promises made to the Fathers: but corrects it until eternity, so that he may take it away according to the idolatry of Solomon, who persevered in his own sin. breaks it or does it not break it, if Solomon is not now good or bad among the sons? But what he says: "True, I will not take all the kingdom": he returns to the species, beginning another figure of Solomon's son and servant. The future body shows: but in this place only evil. The people sinned, he says, and transgressed the covenant that I had arranged for them, they stole from the anathema, they sent their vessels (Jos. 8:11): when only Achard of the tribe of Judah had done this. That the body always understands the future, Jesus said, when he was about to kill him: May God destroy you as he has done today (Ibid., 25). But it is much more necessary to know that: all the cities of Israel and the Gentiles, or the provinces which the Scripture addresses, or in which something has been done, are a figure of the Church. Some parts are indeed bad, some are good, and some are both. For it is impossible to speak the law, which is not in the law: to speak of him, but not to him: and if anywhere without that occasion he addresses foreigners especially in Israel, they are to be believed in the same way: because, even if what was prophesied came to pass, it is still the Church. it is not suitable for all types. For Damascus and Tire and Tire and many others now exist, which God had said to be completely removed and not restored. Esau, and in Dagon, which is the idol of the Allophites, understood that there was a parable against Jerusalem and the temple. The word of the Lord came to me. The Lord: Behold, I will kindle a fire in you, and it will eat up every green tree and every woody thing in you. The burning flame shall not be extinguished, and let it burn every face from the basement to the north, so that all flesh may know that I am the Lord of kindling it, and it shall not be extinguished any more. And I said, no, Lord. They say to me: Is not this that is said a parable (Ez. 20:45, 49)? Jerusalem, looking at their holy places: and you will prophesy over the land of Israel. Thus says the Lord: Behold, I will raise my sword from its scabbard: and I will scatter from you the enemy and the unjust. I am the Lord, who has drawn my sword from its sheath, it will not come out anymore. Set your face, he says, on Teman and look at Dagon (Ez. 21:1, 5). And he interpreted it as saying: Strengthen your face to Jerusalem and look at the holy ones. And he pointed to all Jerusalem, saying: I will scatter from you the enemy and the unjust. Thus, he says about the future in general: So my sword will go out on all flesh from the basement to the north. He shows that in Jerusalem is Theman, whom God kills there, and Dagon, and all the abominable works of the nations, David Solomon in his sons, who also threw down the temples of God and demolished them, and spiritually rebuilt them, threw them into the torrent, that is, the century in which David's son Josiah is born, to be broken up in Bethel, as it is written: Altar, altar, says the Lord, Behold, a son will be born from the house of David: Josiah will be his name (3 Kings 13:2). Nineveh, a city of foreigners, is a figure of the two-part Church. it will be enough that he cannot say that it specifically meets. Nineveh, he says, was a great city (Jonah 3:3): so much so, since it was opposed to God, as the metropolis of the Assyrians, which also destroyed Samaria, and always oppressed all Judea: but in the figure of the Church preaching Jonah, that is, to Christ, she was completely freed. The same Nineveh is described as completely destroyed by the following Prophet, to whom the Lord preached: It is the sign of Jonah in the womb (Matt. 12:40; Luke 11:30). And as the Prophet himself shows that it is not a special city, he interposes some things that exceed the limits of the specific. It was not, he says, the end of the Gentiles: since it was a city of one nation. And again: You have multiplied your merchandise above the stars of heaven, that is, the Church. And again: On whom does not your malice always come? Could the malice of one city, on every man, or ever come, except that which Cain founded with his brother's blood in the name of his son, that is, posterity? The Prophet still teaches more manifestly, and he will stretch out his hand to the north (that is, the people of the sun against the south) and destroy Assyria (Soph. 2:13). all the beasts of the earth, and the camel, and the goats shall lie down in its roofs, and they shall give voice to beasts in its ditches, and ravens in its gates, because the cedar is its height. me (Ibid., 13, 15). She did not receive discipline, she did not trust in the Lord, and she did not draw near to her Lord. His judges, like the wolves of Arabia, do not leave him unarmed. His prophets, lifted up in spirit, despise men. But the righteous Lord will not do unrighteousness in his temple. Egypt is also divided into two parts. Behold, he says, the Lord sits on a light cloud, and he comes into Egypt (Isa. 19:1, 3). Clouds, body it is spiritual after Baptism, and the brightness of the son of man. For the first is the coming of the Lord, coming in his body, as he says: "You shall see him coming in the clouds of heaven." His brother and man, his neighbor, and city will fight against city, and nation will rise against nation (Matt. 24:30), that is, Egypt against Egypt, and law against law, that is, the sense of diversity under one law: And the spirit of the Egyptians will be troubled within them, and their thoughts I will scatter. And after he had now mingled the species with the species, now the species with the species, he added, saying: "And on that day the Lord shall rise up in the land of the Egyptians, and let us declare his title to the Lord. And it shall be a sign to the Lord forever, in the land of the Egyptians" (Is. 19:19). He said: it may be permitted to have an altar at the borders of Egypt eternally: but it will be. But Ezekiel shows more openly that the whole world is Egypt, saying: O day! for the day of the Lord is near, the day of the cloud, the end of the nations: and the sword will come upon the Egyptians. there will be an uproar in Ethiopia, and Egypt will be wounded, and its foundations will fall, the Persians, the Cretans, and the Lydians, and all the foreigners, and the children of my covenant, will fall in it with the sword with them (Ez. 30.3-5). After the exodus they descended into Egypt and were killed there by Nebuchadnezzar according to Jeremiah's prophecy. And it will happen in general, on the last day, when the children of the Egyptians will break the covenant, living in the manner of the Egyptians. Therefore, in Ezekiel, God threatens the king of the Egyptians, and his multitude, because they would be terrible among the saints, appointed among the circumcised: which is not fitting, except those who flatter themselves by circumcision, that is, they flatter themselves as sacred. Because then he gave his fear above life: that he should sleep in the midst of the uncircumcised, wounded by the sword of Pharaoh, and all his multitude with him, says the Lord. says the Lord: I will surround you above the earth of many peoples and I will draw you out in my man and I will spread you over your fields: and I will set all the birds of the sky over you, and I will saturate all the beasts of the whole earth: and I will give your flesh on the mountains, I will saturate the hills with your blood, and the earth will be watered from those that proceed from you; from your multitude I will fill the mountains with briars from you, and I will cover the sky when you are extinguished, and I will darken its stars, I will cover the sun in a cloud, and the light of the moon will not shine. : And I will be angry with many peoples: when I bring your captivity to the nations, to a land that you did not know (Ez. 32:4-8). their face shall be in the midst of them in the day of thy downfall. And I will destroy all the cattle with much water: and the foot of man shall no more be disturbed, and the footsteps of the cattle shall not tread upon it. , and the earth will be desolate with its fullness, and I will scatter those who dwell in it (Ibid., 15).Genus: And they will know that I am the Lord. all that shines with light in heaven will be darkened over you: and I will put darkness on your land (Ez. 32:7, 8). awaiting their downfall from the day of its downfall. For it is also written about Soor: Thus says the Lord to Soor: Is it not, in your days, in the groaning of the wounded, while they are slain by the sword, in your midst the islands will be shaken, and all the princes of the sea will depart from their abodes and will take you away? and the clothing of their ears. of yours (Ez. 26:15-18). At the cry of your voice, your pilots will be afraid, and all your sailors and passengers and sea nets will stand on the ground, and will howl over you with their voice, and will cry bitterly over you , and they shall lay the earth upon their heads, and they shall spread the ashes, and they shall receive upon them the lamentation of the children, the lamentation of Soor. and all thy congregation in the midst of thee. All thy sailors have fallen: all that dwell in the islands are grieved over thee, and they are astonished at the alienation of the minds of the sailors, and their faces are tearful upon thee. (Ez. 27:28-36). It is said to Isaiah, who after many kinds and kinds, also added this, saying: After seventy years, Tire will be like the song of a fornicator. God will do to Tire and it will be restored again as it was before (Is. 23:15-17). What is the use of prophesying that Tire will trade with all the kingdoms of the earth, if not Tire is the Church, in which all earthly business is of eternal life? For it is not collected in them: but in those who dwell in the presence of the Lord. All his business, eating and drinking and being filled, as a sign of remembrance in the sight of the Lord (Ibid. 18). If then his business is holy to the Lord: how can for it follows clearly, he shows what Tire is, saying: Behold, the Lord will destroy the earth, and will waste it, and will lay bare its face: he will scatter those who dwell in it, and the people will be like a priest (Is. 24:1-6). and he mourned, as he who mourns: for the earth shall be corrupted by corruption, and the earth shall be laid waste by desolation. This is what the Lord has spoken. and they have changed the commandments of the eternal testament. Because of this, therefore, the curse eats up the earth: because those who dwell in it have sinned. Because of this, those who dwell in the earth will be numerous (Is. 24:1-6). the trade is to eat, to drink, and to fill, not at a certain time, but as a sign of remembrance in the sight of the Lord? And few men will be left. The vine will mourn, the wine will mourn. lyres? They were confused: they did not drink the pure wine, it became bitter for those who drank it. The land will be desolate in the midst of the nations. If every city is deserted; What are the nations in whose midst they make a mediator? Although some of these seem to be invisible, all are spiritual. He says that every city is deserted and spiritually dead: but of that harlot of Tyre, not whose traffic is in the holy world. A few will be left of them, whom he calls spiritually dead: those who lived by remembrance, whom Ecclesiasticus did not kill: as we read in many places. to Syria or to the stubble, after a little while, the fire will come. He will send, says the Lord of hosts, for your honor and dishonor: and for your brightness, a burning fire: and Israel will burn as a light, and it will be a fire for you, and he will sanctify it in a burning flame (of course, the light of Israel), and he will eat like hay, a forest. and those who remain of them shall be numbered, and a child shall write them (Is. 10:16-19). Those who remain, he says, of them. We have written to Zechariah, to rescue those whom the Church will not kill, that they may turn to themselves: but to kill the rest spiritually by crucifixions. For if they stand still, let their eyes be blinded, and their flesh burn: He shall dwell, he says, trusting in Israel; Their flesh shall perish as they stand under their feet: their gills shall flow from their holes, and their tongue shall perish in their mouth. leading a blind man). that destruction. The Lord: I will break the bow of Nair, their dominion in Elam. of them, and I will overcome them according to the wrath of my indignation, and I will send my sword after them, until it consumes them. It is written: Hear the word of the Lord, princes of Sodom (Is. 1:10), and what is spiritually called Sodom and Egypt: where also the Lord's people were crucified (Rev. 11:8). of sin (2 Thess. 2:3). Babylon the city against Jerusalem: the whole world is on its side, as Israel is here. These agree: A vision, he says, against Babylon, and he says against the whole world, the holy soldiers of God who will come: Take away the vice and rejoice over them, do not fear, exhort; open the hands of the magistrates: for behold, I command. The giants are sanctified and called; they come, rejoicing in my wrath at the same time and doing insults. And he overthrew the king of the Medes. He followed them and said, "Who are these kings, and what is Babylon?" Because of this all hands will be broken, and every soul of man will tremble. (Ibid., 4-9). and it will be dark, and the light will not continue. And those who remain (that is, those whom the aforesaid soldiers did not kill) will be honored more than gold, which does not touch the fire, and man will be honored more than a sapphire stone. whatever his indignation may be. and if those who are gathered shall fall by the sword, and their daughters shall fall before them, and their houses shall be plundered, and their wives shall be taken. All things are written spiritually, as of the same Babylon: Blessed is he who prevails and dashes his little ones to the rock and the sons of Babylon collide at the rock of stumbling. Obtaining that, as it is written: He who conquers only, let him hold, until he is in the midst (2 Thess. 2:7). on her mountains, that is to destroy the Church. This is what the Lord says: I will make Babylon desolate, so that the heathen will inhabit it, and it will come to naught, and I will make it a desolate place for destruction. So will it continue, that I may destroy the Assyrians in the land and in my mountains, and they shall be trampled upon, their yoke shall be broken from them, and the glory shall be taken away from the Humerites. For what the holy God has planned, who will disperse it and who will turn away that strong hand (Isa. 14:22-27)? And every time after the destruction threatens the ruin of the city, the dwelling of the beasts, the unclean spirits say that they will dwell in the unpeople whom the Holy Spirit has abandoned. , to feel the morning. The sermons (says Amos) which he saw over Jerusalem, and he began. I will not turn it into four, because he persecuted his brother with the sword (Ibid., 11). And he meets many other alien communities in the figure of the Church. Wherever he mentions Idumaea, Theman, Bosor, Seir, it means bad brothers. But they are the possessions of Esau. He says: men are hard and harsh, who cut off the churches that give birth. Also: all the nations that are under heaven will drink the wrath of God in the city of God and be smitten there. the nations to whom I am sending you: and they will vomit and become mad because of the sword that I am sending in the midst of them. in desolation, and in desolation, and in hissing, and Pharaoh, king of Egypt, and his children, and his servants, all his people, and all his promiscuous people, all the nations of the foreigners, Ashkelon, and Gaza, and Akkaron, and those that are against Azoth, and Idumaea, and Moabite , and the children of Ammon, and the king of Tyre, and the king of Sidon, and the kings that are beyond the sea, and Dedan, and Teman, and Bosor, and all that are round about from the face, and all the promiscuous ones that dwell in the wilderness, and all the kings of Elam, and all the kings of the Persians, and all the kings from subsolano, those who are far and those who are near, each one to his brother, and all the kingdoms of the earth that are on the face of the earth, and you shall say to them: Thus says the Lord Almighty: Drink and get drunk, and vomit, and fall and rise from the face of the sword, which I will send in the middle And to those who refused to accept the cup, so that they were drinking, you will say: Thus says the Lord: You will drink, because in the city in which my name is invoked, I will begin to afflict you upon it: and you will not be cleansed by cleansing, because I will call a sword upon the inhabitants of the earth (Jer. 25, 15-29) You shall drink, he says, Jerusalem, the cities of Judah, and their kings and their princes. Then he says: And all the kingdoms of the earth that are on the face of the earth: to show that he had made the transition from the particular Jerusalem to the general, in where are all the nations of the earth whom God will smite there, just as he interpreted, saying: As for the city in which my name is invoked, I will begin to afflict you, and you will not be cleansed by purification. if he had not been drawn, they would have gone to Egypt. in the principal part of them. If anything, especially Satan, if anything heavy, if anything, he has the right hand of his body: he has mingled with the heavenly, as he is the most warlike, to oppose the strong with the strong. Whence the Apostle says, that the saints do not fight against humanity, but against spiritual wickedness in the heavenly (Eph. 6:12).

Rule V

Of the Times.

The quantity of times in the Scriptures is frequently mystical by the trope of synecdoche; or with legitimate numbers, which are placed in many ways, and for the place of understanding. Synecdochevero, it is either a part of the whole, or a part of the whole. In this trope, Israel served 400 years in Egypt. not their own, and they will rule over them and afflict them for 400 years (Gen. 15:13). And the Scriptures of Exodus say: He was in Egypt for 430 years (Ex. 12:40). Did he not serve all the time? For the Scripture says that he did not serve the people until after the death of Joseph, and of all his brothers, and of all the generations. Joseph was ignorant, and said to his people: Behold, the nation of the children of Israel is a great multitude, and they are strong above us. Come, then, let us surround them (Exodus 1:7-10). delayed, we deduce 80 years of Joseph's reign (for he reigned from 30 years to 110) the rest of Israel's servitude will be 340 years, which God said was 400. But if he served Israel all the time of his pilgrimage, it is more than God said. If from the death of Joseph according to the faith of the Holy Scriptures, it is less. For it is evident that 100 is a part of the whole. months: the first day of the month is the 10th, as it is written: I was formed in the womb of the mother for 10 months, flesh congealed in blood. The remains of the millions are a thousand years. Six days are the age of the world, that is, 6000 years. is, three hours, a whole day, one of the three burials of the Lord: thus, the remains of the sixth said elder, whom the Church raised, is a whole day, a thousand years. For this trope, there are three days and three chains. Nights are added to days, except for a certain reason. We say otherwise, days only, as the apostle is said to have remained with Peter. Was it necessary to say, as many days and nights? Is one time: the last hour of the day, and it keeps the whole day and the night passed. Similarly, and the last hour of the night, the whole day and the future night. For the hour is a part of both times. When he arose, part of the day was approaching. Furthermore, if the past did not fall in the present day, nor in the night of the present day tomorrow, the Lord did not rise in the day, but in the night.). But the Lord rose before the sun rose. For Mark says: In the east of the sun (Matt. 16:2), not at the rising, but in the east, that is, at the rising: but Luke, early (Luke 24:1). For Matthew said that the women went to the tomb at night and saw the Lord (Matt. 28:1). But John, when it was still dark (John 20:1). But if the Lord was before the sun, that is, before the beginning of the day arose, that night was a part of the shining day. And it behooves the works of God, that the day should not be darkened into night, but that the night should shine into the day. He said: Let light shine in our hearts out of darkness (II Cos. 4:6). He who enlightened the darkness, as it is written: Your darkness will be like the south (Is. 58:10). And: The night has passed, but the day is near as we walk decently in the day (Rom. 13:12). For what is carnal is first, then what is spiritual. Therefore, the first and the last day are part of the whole. Only the middle was full, from evening to evening, according to the condition and the precept. From evening to evening I darkened the Sabbath day (Lev. 23:33). Some say that it should be counted from the day: because the Lord said three days and nights, not three nights and days. But this is not destroyed by a long argument. The end of the burial is in the night: but if it ended in the day, it began from the night. For if the day is concluded on both sides, there will be one more day. They say, moreover, that it is not possible for the day to be the past night, nor for the night to be the future day: three separate days and nights must be assigned, counting the first day on which he was crucified: the second, three hours repaired, the third Sabbath, will be the Lord's Day. the second on the Sabbath, the third on Sunday. The nights are indeed three, but the days are two. it is necessary to agree that the rest of the Friday was a past night. If the darkness was intrusive, yet the three hours of the light are of the same day: they did not lose their order, since they were part of their day and night. of God's condition. For whatever is a sign, it does not disturb the reasonable course of the elements. The days of the night were subtracted, or added, and from there began a new reckoning of the seasons or of the seasons, which God established in the sun and the moon, to be the days and years of the seasons, as it is written in Genesis (Gen. 1, 17). Much more on that day, nothing was disturbed, to which 3 hours of darkness had not been added, so that they were 15. Certainly, if the contention can be calmed at all by reason, we summarily prove that the 3 hours of darkness do not belong to the burial of the Lord, because he was still alive. Because after sunset, it was not permitted for the Jews to bury: when the meal was pure the beginning of the Sabbath, as John says (John 13:2; 19, 42). There, therefore, because of the pure supper of the Jews, since he had been the neighbor, they placed Jesus in the tomb. That all males are the firstborn, as it is said: He begat sons and daughters and died (Gen. 5). What happens against the law of nature, that all those males begot first. But for us all time is a day. All things are new, the figures have passed away. They are in numbers, a seven-denarius, a denarius, a twelve-denarius. But the number is the same when it is multiplied: as seventy, or seven hundred, or as many times in itself: as seven times seven, or ten thousand. But they either signify perfection, or the whole separately, or a simple sum. as seven spirits. The seven churches (Rev. 1, 4-11). Or as he says: Seven times a day I will send you down (Ps. 168, 164): or he will only receive seven times in this age (Matt. 22; Eccl. 35, 13). Similarly, a denarius, as another Evangelist says: He will only receive a hundredfold in this age (Mark 10:30). Dan.7:10), And David: God's chariot, he says, only a million times (Ps. 67:18) And of all time, David: for a thousand centuries (Ps.54:8). is 144,000 and twelve three (Rev. 7:4, 5), all the nations, as: Judiciable twelve tribes of Israel (Matt. 19:28). Apart from the whole: since a hundred times is defined by legitimate numbers, as in the Apocalypse: You will have pressure for 10 days (Rev. 4:10): since it means until infinity. The Septuagint before in Babylon, that it was the same time, it is importunate to prove now. Besides the legitimacy of numbers, the scripture has frequently shortened any time in any number, as the aforementioned time, called the Hour, saying to the Apostle: It is the last hour (1 John 2:18). 2). For not he to whom the Lord preached was alone acceptable: but also he to whom he preaches, as it was said: I have heard thee in due time (Is. 49, 8); and the Apostle is interpreted: Behold, now is an acceptable time (II Cor. 6, 2). Finally, the end of this year, that is, he joined the judgment, saying: To preach the acceptable year of the Lord, and the day of retribution. 64, 12. Sometimes an hour, days, and months is a year, as in the Apocalypse: Be prepared for an hour, a day, and a month, one year (Rev. 9, 15), that is, three years and a half. Ibid, months for years: It was given to him to destroy the people, five months (Ibid., 5). Sometimes, the number of days is 100 days, as in the Apocalypse: One thousand two hundred and sixty days (Rev. 11, 3); for there are six thousand two hundred and sixty-one hundred and six thousand days, which are three hundred and fifty years, in months of three hundred days. There are those who are three hundred and fifty years. The time is the same year, or 100 years: as time, and times, and half a time (Dan. 7:25; 12:7), which is, or 3 years and a half, or 350. Also: One day is sometimes a hundred years; as it is written of the Church: He shall lie in the city, where his Lord also was from the crucifixion, and after three days and a half (Rev. 11:8, 11). and after three days to rise again (Matt. 20:18; Mark 10:33; Luke 18:32). For he himself rose again on the third day. Generations are several times and a hundred years: as the Lord says to Abraham: But the fourth generation will return here (Gen. 15:16). In Exodus, however, it is said not of slavery, but of the time of the entire pilgrimage: And in the fifth generation, the people came up from Egypt (Ex. 12:42), that is, after 430 years. The same generation, sometimes, is 10 years: like Jeremiah says: You will be in Babylon until seven generations (Bar. 6:2). ten (Luke 19:13): he reduces the ten to three, while he himself says the exact reason for the three. The first seven days are 7000 years. God worked for six days and rested from all his work on the seventh day, and blessed and sanctified the little one (Ibid., 2, 3). In the same way, this world worked in six days: the spiritual world, which is the Church, works for 6000 years, and will stop on the seventh day, which he blessed and made for eternity. he does, he loves the Sabbath of God: that is, the seventh day of eternal rest. For this reason God exhorts the people not to enter the gates of Jerusalem on the Sabbath day, and threatens the gates, and those who enter and exit through them, as Jeremiah commands, saying: Go, these are in the gates of the children of your people , into which the kings of Judah enter and go out, and in all the gates of Jerusalem, and you shall say to them: Hear the word of the Lord, you who enter these gates. Do not carry burdens from your houses on the Sabbath day, as I commanded your fathers. on the sabbath day, so that you do not face all your work, and sanctify the sabbath day, and the kings and princes of this city will enter through the gates of this city, sitting on the seat of David. forever, and they will come from the cities of Judah, and from the cities of Jerusalem, and from the land of Benjamin, and from the land of the plain, and from the land to the south, bringing burnt offerings and incense, and manna, and frankincense, bringing praise in the house of the Lord. And if you will not hear me that ye may sanctify the Sabbath day, that ye may not carry burdens, nor enter through the gates of Jerusalem: a fire shall be kindled in the gates thereof, and shall consume the houses of Jerusalem, and shall not be quenched (Jer. 17:19-27). to bring burdens through the gates of Jerusalem? Or, if it were necessary: and he would say the type of work, that is, do not bring burdens through the gates. For some did not bring burdens into the city through the walls and roofs, and through them he is cursed. But those who enter through the gates, enter into the eternal. of many, with booths in the holy city (Is. 56:20). Christ is the gate of the holy city, Jerusalem, and his deputies, the guardians of the law: killing the true prophets and stoning those sent to him. hiding in a deep sense. They are the gates that do not overcome the church, which is founded on the rock. He enters through Christ. For he himself has the precepts, he expounds them to his onlookers, and without him he does not enter into the rest of the sabbath. But if anyone enters not through the precepts, but through the deeds of those who preside over the seat of

Moses, he is a son of hell more than they are. let him be found with his burden on the Sabbath day, on which there is no manna to be gathered, nor burden to be laid. Because they want to hear the voice of the Son of God crying out to the Church and saying: Come to me, all you who labor and are heavy laden, and I will give you rest (Matt. 11:28). These are the thieves who enter their Jerusalem not through the true door, but through their gates. other commandments of the law are a figure of the future Thus, he says: "Therefore let no one judge you, and I may be called either on the part of the feast, or on the Sabbath, or on the Sabbath: which is a shadow of the future" (Col. 2:16). They made two periods to be described separately, as if they were not sequential. Joseph, lord of Egypt, became a figure when he was 30 years old. Which are therefore for us seven years of fertility and satiety: the same for the other seven of barrenness and famine. For at that time the Lord threatens famine to the rich, but satiety to the poor. and the evils of a double time coming at one time. The writing of Exodus testifies (Ex. 10), because it is evident that Israel was immune from all the plagues of Egypt and had light during the three days of darkness. This is now being done spiritually, as God himself later threatened Pharaoh, saying: I will bring darkness over your land (Ibid. 2). Each one of which is a time. Thus, the year in which Noah was incarcerated is divided into all numbers. However, whenever there is a mention of time, the quaternary number is specifically the time from the passion of the Lord to infinity. Now it is quaternary, whenever it is full, or after the third part of the fourth, as 340 or three days and a half. But the rest (for they are to be understood as places) are signs, not clear definitions. Forty days of the flood is the whole time. There were 40 years in Egypt, and 40 years in the wilderness, and 40 days of fasting of the Lord and Moses and the same 40 days in which the Church eats and drinks with the Lord after the resurrection are 40 years in which the Church was eating and drinking under Solomon, in deep peace on every side, yet oppressing them with the two-parted Solomon: as the same Church says: The Father oppressed us one time (3 Kings 12, 30). For forty days, the water was in its state, and it failed as many times as possible: so that twice and the failure of the water in 10 months, that is, it was completed at the perfect time. Then he fails. Because at the same time he is healthy carnally, at the same time he fails spiritually, so that the exaltation itself is a failure, until the time is completed. Thus, the reigning world is placed under the feet of the Church, the son of man. Which are therefore 40 days, the sins of Judah and Israel are 149, which is one and the same. The ark sat in the 7th month, the same time: And the water failed until the 10th month, the same time. It came out of the ark in the 12th month (Gen. 7:14). of this year, it is the same year. As he said, he came out of the Ark on the fortieth day, or on the 7th or 10th of the month.

Rule VI

Of the recapitulation.

These parts are recapitulations from the beginning to the end: like Adam until Enoch, that is, the translation of the Church, seven generations, that is, all time. Again, from Adam to Noah, that is, repair, ten generations, which is all time: and from Noah to Abraham ten generations. He is governed by a flood that reaches the whole world. We leave the given way to be more fully investigated by the prudent. Because there would not be enough to interpret the Scriptures; to pursue each detail, and even those things which might hinder this understanding, we thought not to be removed, while hastening to another. Among the rules which the spirit has sealed with the law: by which the way of light should be kept, some recapitulation keeps the seal with such subtlety, that the continuation of the narrative is seen rather than a recapitulation. For sometimes he recapitulates thus: Then at that hour, at that day, at that time; as the Lord speaks in the Gospel, saying: On the day that Lot came out of Sodom, fire rained down from heaven and destroyed them all (Gen. 19:24). According to these things, there will be the days of the son of man (Matt. 24:37), when that prayer will be revealed, he who is on the roof, and his vessels in the house, will not take them down, and he who is in the field will not turn back in the same way (Matt. 13:15, 16). He remembers Lot's wife (Luke 17:32). At that hour, when the Lord was revealed at his coming, should not one have turned and remembered the abodes that are his, and Lot's wife, and that he should be revealed before? And the Lord at that hour, having been troubled, commanded that these things should be observed: not only by concealing them would he make the truth more agreeable to those who sought it; And so, at the same hour, that is, at the time, he ordered these things to be observed: but before it was revealed. The same hour, indeed, but in what part of the hour is recognized. Sometimes, however, there are not recapitulations of this kind, but future similitudes, as the Lord says: When you see what was said by Daniel the prophet, then those who are in Judea will flee to the mountains (Matt. 24:15; Dan. 9:27). And it brings the end. And what Daniel said: It is done in Africa, and the end is not at the same time. But since it will not be in that title. Therefore, he said, that is, when the same thing happened throughout the world: which is the departure and revelation of man's sin. This is the kind of expression the Spirit says in the Psalms. Then they will say to those who died, the Lord has magnified what he has done with them. The Lord has magnified what he has done with us: we have become rejoicing (Ps. 25:1-3). Indeed, saying: When the Lord turned away from the captivity of Zion: then they said among the nations. Now he will turn away, he says. Then they will say among the nations. Let us know the nations whose captivity he averts. Like their figure, we have a time saying: The Lord magnified to do with them, the Lord magnified to do with us. Therefore, concerning the similitude of his time and ours, he made one thing and joined it, saying: Then they will say among the nations, that is, when he did the same to the nations. Many pseudo-prophets came into this world after John. In this know the spirit of God. Every spirit that looses Jesus, and denies that he came in the flesh, is not of God, but this one is of Antichrist. That which you have heard is coming and is now present in this world (1 John 4:3). Does everyone who does not deny that Jesus came in the flesh have the Spirit of God? But this negation is to be in the work, not in the voice, and that each one must be understood not from his profession, but from his fruits: in every Epistle which he wrote only about the fruits of good and evil, he subtly reminds us, in the same kind of expression, as he says: In this we shall know, if we keep his precepts (1 John 2, 3, 4). But he who says: Because I know him and does not keep his commandments, is a liar. Is it understood by profession that a brother who does not know God, and does not expose himself? And whoever says that he loves God and hates his brother is a liar (1 John 4:20). Sienim, as he says, loves God: let him teach by works, adhere to God, love God in his brother. If he believes Christ incarnate; let him cease to hate the members of Christ. If he believes the Word made flesh, why does he pursue the flesh, the Word made flesh (John 1:14) Why pursue the word in the flesh? What the Lord said: As long as you did it to one of the least of my brothers who believed in me, you did it to me (Matt. 25:40): not an operetta in Christ's flesh, that is, in his servants, since the Lord and the Church are one flesh. In what way does he believe that he is a man: why does he not love, or what is crueler, why does he hate, as it is written: He who does not love his brother remains in death (1 John 3:14). And he who hates his brother is a murderer (Ibid., 14). He said that there is no other greater and more evident sign of knowing the Antichrist, than that he who denies in the flesh hates his brother? And such as he says: Because he who denies Christ in the flesh is not of God (2 John 17): such as, No one can say Lord Jesus, except in the Holy Spirit (1 Cor. 12:3). Not all who say to me, Lord, Lord, will enter the kingdom of heaven (Matt. 7:21). But in this the Apostle, that no one can say the Lord

Jesus Christ, unless he said in the Holy Spirit according to his conscience (1 Cor. 12:3), according to the inner man, not according to a mere profession, he would point out to those who say Lord Jesus, to have none the less from those who are exalted by different kinds of charisma. But everyone who believes in the Lord Jesus possesses one and the same Spirit. No one, he says, can say the Lord Jesus, except in the Holy Spirit. And there are divisions of ministries: and the same Lord (Ibid., 4, 5). But to break Jesus, is not to do what Jesus confesses to have done, as the same Lord says: Whoever breaks one of these least commandments, and thus teaches men, he will be called the least in the kingdom of heaven (Matt. 5:20). And when he has resolved what it is, he opens it up to those who follow, saying: But he who did it, taught it thus. Therefore, this denial, that it is of works, not of words, and the Apostle Paul confirms it, saying: They confess that they know the Lord, but they deny it by deeds (Tit. 1:16). And again: having a form of godliness but denying its virtue (II Tim. 3:5). In this sense he says, brethren, that Christ should not be preached with a holy voice, but with the heart. For they preach with a holy voice. And he consented to their preaching, and ordered them to be heard, saying: What difference does it make whether Christ be announced by occasion or by truth (Philip. 1:18). By tending to another, he enters by the name of Christ: by which he paves the way for himself, by which under the name of Christ, he prepares his belly, and to these (which is shameful to say), he imposes the name of holiness and simplicity, asserting that the works of the chambers of signs and wonders are Christ. abstain yourselves from idols (1 John 5:21).

Rule VII

Of the devil and his body.

Two passages are illustrated, Isaiah chapter 14, and Ez. 28. Of the devil and his body it can be seen briefly, if what was said of the Lord and his body is also observed. In Isaiah, the king of Babylon, it is said: How did Lucifer fall from heaven, rising in the morning? He was crushed on the earth, who was sent to all the nations? above the clouds, I will be like the Most High. But now you have descended to the underworld, to the foundations of the earth. All the kings of the nations had slept in honor in their homes. But you were thrown into the mountains as dead, abhorred with all those who fell by the sword in the wilderness and went down to hell. How did you come: as a garment sprinkled with blood will not be clean, so neither will you be clean, because the earth you have destroyed mine, and you have killed my people. You will not be a wicked seed forever, prepare, kill your children, do not let the sin of your father rise again (Is. 19:12, 22). for it is a body. How, he says, did Lucifer fall from heaven, rising in the morning, and broken upon the earth: who is sent to all nations? to be able to ascend, who was not able to resist. And if he dwells above the stars, to make himself like God, even the Scripture itself reminds us to inquire. He has a seat of this kind. Heaven, he says, the Church: as we shall see as the Scriptures proceed. Rev. 22:16). Also there: He who overcomes, let the morning star shine (Rev. 2, 28): that is, that the morning star may be like Christ, whom we received. Lucifer is therefore a part, that is, against the body, which is the devil, kings, and the people, fall from heaven, and let the earth be crushed. Wisdom says of these rules: I will listen, kings, and understand: learn to judge the ends of the earth, lend ears, who contain the multitude, and you will be pleased in the multitudes of the nations: for you have been given power from the Lord, and strength from Most high; who will question your works, and will search your thoughts. Because, when you were the ministers of that kingdom, you did not judge righteously, nor did you keep the law (Wis. 6, 2, 3). Therefore, the king of Babylon is the whole body: but for the places we understand, into which part of the body he falls. from heaven, lucifer can come into everybody. Let me ascend into heaven, let me set my seat upon the stars of God, likewise, and my head: the greater ones, who think they are lords of the stars of God, that is, the saints, while they are lording over their lesser ones, as it is written: The greater shall serve the lesser. To this Esau, that is, to the evil brothers, thus says the

Lord through Obadiah the prophet: Exalting his habitation, saying in his heart: Who brought me down to the earth? says the Lord (Ob. 1:3, 4). They make a union, that is, the body of the devil. If the mountains are evil, the Scripture says: The mountains will be transferred into the heart of the sea (Ps. 45:3). Again: The foundations of the mountains are disturbed and moved, because God is angry. For the body of the Lord, that is, the Church, is called a mountain: and each one who is the Church, makes mountains, as it is written: "I have been established as a king by him, on Zion the holy mountain, announcing his dominions" (Ps. 2:6). And again, I will destroy the Assyrians in my land and in my mountains (Is. 14:25). (Ps. 13:4). God has his seat in Mount Zion, and in the mountains of Israel, and in his holy clouds: which is the Church). Again, I will command the clouds, let them rain down upon her (Isa. 5, 6)., dwelling in Zion, my holy mountain (Ez. 35:3). And the devil will sit in the mountains, but Seir, who is Esau, that is, the evil brothers: which mountain God rebukes through Ezekiel and says that in the joy of the whole earth he will desolate, because of enmity against Israel He is a mountain, the mountains of the North. In these the devil sits; and he dominates the clouds of heaven. So far, he says that he is like the Most High (Is. 14:14). There are two parts in the Church, the East and the North, that is, the South and the North. In the South part, the Lord remains. It is written: Where you feed, where you stay in the south (Cant. 1:6)? But the devil, in the north, as God says to his people: I will pursue him from the north for you, and I will drive him out into a land without water, that is, without water; and I will exterminate his face in the first sea, and his hindquarters in the last sea, which is the first and last of the unpeopled (Joel. 11:10). This world was built in the likeness of the Church, in which the Solorians, not except through the South, that is, has a meridian; and having run through the southern part, he goes back to his place invisible. So also, our Lord Jesus Christ, the eternal sun travels in his direction, whence he also calls the meridian. But with the eagle, that is, it does not rise on the opposite side. it shines upon us. But for those who fear the Lord, the Sun of righteousness rises and healing is in his wings, as it is written (Mal. 4:2). But evil is the night at noon: as it is written: While they themselves endure the light, darkness is made to the slivers, they walked in the light of the dark night, they groped like a blind man against a wall, and he who has no eyes, groped and fell at noon, as if in the middle of the night (Is. 69:9, 10). of light (Amos 8:9). Again: Therefore, night will be for you from vision, and darkness will be for you from divination, and the sun will kill the super-prophets, and the day of light will darken over them (Mich. 3:6). God threatens these people from the South, as through Ezekiel he rebukes Soor, saying: The Spirit of the East has crushed you (Ez. 27:16). For he allows them to crush you, saying: Arise, North, and come, South: blow your garden, and the perfumes will flow down (Song 4:16). The spirit resists the Holy Spirit, who pervades the garden of the Lord, and perfumes are drawn out, that is, a sweet smell is offered. Upon thee Gog, the prince of Mosoch and Tobel: and I will gather thee, and bring thee, and set thee at the end of the North, and bring upon thee the mountain of Israel: and I will destroy the bow from thy left hand, and the arrows from the right hand, and I will cast thee upon the mountains of Israel (Ez. 39:1-4). And this is carried out by the passion of the Lord, until the Church departs from the midst of the mystery of the perpetrator, which holds back, so that impiety may be revealed in due time, as the Apostle says: And now you know what she holds back, so that it may be revealed in her own time: the mystery for he is already working iniquity: so much so that he who detains only detains, until he becomes of the midst. And then the wicked will be revealed (2 Thess. 2:6-8). these words to the north, and say: Turn to me, house of Israel, says the Lord (Jer. 3:3). But the south is part of the Lord; as it is written in Job: From the southern part life will sprout (Job. 11, 17). With the eagle of the devil: And both sides, in the whole world. I will ascend, says he, the clouds: I will be like the Most High. But now let the foundations of the earth descend to hell. Those who see you, they will be amazed at you and will say: This is a man who stirs up the earth, shakes kings, who makes the whole world of the earth desolate. Does it agree with the devil? Those who see you will be amazed at you? Or at the last king, when you descend to hell? descending into the underworld, there will be no one to marvel at the end of the world. For they will not say: This is the man who stirred up the earth, the kings, and made the entire world of the earth desolate; when God strikes a part and casts down the underworld, we say: This is the man who stirs up the earth, shakes the kings, that is, the saints: He who lays the burden of the earth all desolate: it is the voice of those who mock, not of those who confirm it, as there: He who destroys the temple, and in three days raises it up (Mark 15:29). For he said: I will make strength, and wisdom of the understanding. He contradicts me (Is. 10:13, 14). Is he able to fulfill those things which he promises himself? He indeed makes the entire world of the earth desolate, but his own world. Let the earth be moved at the face of the Lord. Indeed, he founded the world of the earth, which will not be moved (Ps. 25:9). In truth, they are made and spoken in the form of generality, and they are spiritually filled: while those who dominate, they afflict the subjects of humility, either through temptation or by merit, without respect and common condition, for whom power is not sufficient, but they use it excessively, which they blame, saying : Pursuing retribution (Is. 1:23). And again: He extends his hand to him in retribution (Ps. 14:21). He still behaves and takes revenge on the subject, as it is written: You will punish all your subjects. All the kings of the earth slept in honor, a man in his house (Is. 14:18,19). let us be cast down upon the mountains, as if dead abominated, they fell with all the sword inserted, and descend to the underworld. He says to the devil, 'You are cast upon the mountains whereon he sits.' for as the Lord said, whatever his own suffer, he suffers himself (Matt. 25:40): so also the devil himself is trampled upon in his own, he himself is abhorred and crushed, as it is written: In the diminution of the people, the crushing of the prince (Prov. 14:28) The devil is not separated from his man: nor can a man in whom the devil is not say: I will be like the Most High. Neither can the devil, this man, who incites the earth: unless he was in man. Like the Lord, man cannot be called except in man; I will not die, except in Christ. eternal time, wicked seed: prepare, kill your children with the sins of their fathers, so that they do not rise again (Is. 14:19-21). That is, Nebuchadnezzar died in the world, he lived for eternity: he says to his body that he has begotten those who are ready for each time, let him be killed by his sins, by which he, who is born, will be killed. God rebukes the king of Tyre: Because your heart was exalted, and you said: I am God, I lived in the dwelling of God in the order of the sea. But you are a man, and not God: and you gave your heart as the heart of God. Are you wiser, Daniel? Has your wisdom or your learning made you mighty, and gold and silver your treasures? Have you multiplied your prowess in the abundance of your learning and in your trading? For this reason says the Lord: For I will give you as the heart of God: for this reason, behold, I will bring upon you foreign plagues from among the nations , and they will empty your swords on you, and on the beauty of your doctrine: and they will wound your beauty to destruction, and you will be laid down, and you will die the death of the wounded in the heart of the sea. God. You will perish in the multitude of the uncircumcised, in the hands of strangers: because I have spoken, says the Lord. Sardius, Topaz, Emerald, Carbuncle, and Sapphire, and Jasper, and silver, etaurus, and Ligyrium, and Agate, and this Amethyst, Chrysolithum, and Beryl, and Onychium: and fill your treasures and your storehouses with gold. You went without a spot in your days, from which day you were created, until your iniquities were found in you. You filled the storehouses with your iniquity and sins with the abundance of your traffic: and you were wounded by the mountain of God. Cherubim took you from the midst of the stones of hell, your heart was lifted up in your heart: your doctrine is corrupted with your decorum. Because of the multitude of sins and the immorality of your dealings, the holy ones have been defiled: I will raise up a fire from within you, it will devour you. you. You have become a ruin, and you will not stand forever (Ez. 28:2-19). He meets the man who says: I am the Christ; and in the devil who dwells in the heart of the sea, that is, the people dwell, just as God sits in the heart of his saints. to the city: You are satiated and honored too much in the heart of the sea. In where your sailors brought you many things: the Spirit of the East crushed you in the heart of the sea of your virtue. The devil in a man is called a man: as the Lord said in the Gospel: The enemy of man did this (Matt. 13:28). Therefore, it is appropriate in both: You are a man, and not God. You have given your heart as the heart of God. Are you wiser than Daniel? than the sons of light. It may also agree in a species: since Daniel specially confounds the king of Babylon, into a figure who, with the prophetic spirit, prostrated the proud king to the confession of one God, with Ecclesiastical majesty, who, with confessional virtues and heavenly wisdom, overthrew the superstitions of Babylon. For not only the wise Daniel, but also the three boys, who, by asserting one Lord and the same God, confounded the king and all his kingdom with their gods. Hast thou made thee prowess, and gold and silver thy treasures? Hast thou not much knowledge, or hast thou multiplied thy prowess in thy market? and thy heart is exalted in thy prowess. Not a course for the light, not a battle for the strong, nor bread for the wise (Eccl. 9:11). power, but they are conferred by God. For what do you have that you did not receive? But if you received, why do you boast, as if you did not receive (1 Cor. 4:7)? And again: Let not the wise man glory in his wisdom (Jer. 9:23) Therefore says the Lord: Because you have given your heart as the heart of God: Therefore, behold, I will bring upon you strangers, exterminating plagues: and they shall empty their swords upon you, and the superlative beauty of your knowledge. (Ez. 28:7, 8). It is in power to conform to the appearance that the kings of the world, through persuasive pride, suffer themselves to be called lords; yet this also belongs to the genus. by the like, so Mattathias. And they will wound your beauty to destruction. For some they wound not to destruction, but with hope of health. He is clearly wounded and dies but he is the one in whom he is wounded. Will you say in the presence of those who have done it: I am God? you will perish in the multitude of the uncircumcised of the hands of the aliens: because I have spoken, says the Lord. And the word of the Lord came to me, saying: Son of man, take the lamentation over the prince of Tyre, and say to him: Thus says the Lord: You are a sign of likeness, and a crown of beauty in paradise. , so that he who has lost paradise is reproached? Man was in the delights of paradise, he is a sign of similitude, who was made in the likeness of God. and dry; and I will turn the chariots and the riders. And the horses and their riders will go down, each one with a sword to his brother. In that day, says the Lord Almighty, I will take you Zerubbabel son of Salathiel, a servant, and I will set a sign on you, because I have chosen you, says the Lord Almighty. Zerubbabel, all flesh is (Hag. 2:22-24; Eccl. 49:13). Indeed, from that point on, we never read that Zerubbabel was moved above himself. He was from the tribe of Judah, who under Darius deserved to build Jerusalem. this house, and his hands shall finish it (Zach. 4:9). But this is a sign and a crown of appearance, as God promises to the Church, saying: The nations will see your righteousness, your glory, and they will call on your name, which the Lord has named. That will be the crown of appearance in in the hand of the Lord, and the diadem of the kingdom in the hand of your God. You will not be called desolate, and your land will not be called desolate. and the crown of the species: whose part, in the very beauty of the divine similitude, and the delights of paradise, that is, the church, endures. On the other hand, the part, lest it should live forever, between itself and the tree of life, a flaming sword is drawn out (Gen. 3:24). For Adam, as the apostle says, the shadow will come (Rom. 5:14). So also, these brothers, he was divided into Cain and Abel. Having every best stone bound in you; Sardius, and Topaz, and Emerald, and Carbuncle, and Sapphire, and Jaspin, silver, etaurus, and Liguria, and Achaten, and Amethyst, and Chrysolite, and Beryl, and Onyx: and fill thy treasuries with gold, and thy storehouses in thee. For these twelve stones and gold and silver, all the treasures of the devil's hands are attached to the devil. When you see your children, they are gathered together and come to you. I will live, says the Lord, because you will put them on all of them and put them on them: like the ornaments of a new bride, because your deserts and desolate things, and those that have fallen, will now be distressed by the inhabitants (Is. 49:18, 19; 60:14). And in the Apocalypse, the same city is built on the foundation of twelve stones (Rev. 21:19, 20). Everything, he says, is the best stone, and he enumerated twelve: in order to show perfection in the number of twelve. For everything that he did God, they are good (Gen. 1:25). The devil changed their use, not their nature. Etomnes men of excellent sense and powerful intellect, are gold and silver, and precious stones according to nature: but they will be his in whose obedience, nature, they enjoy theirs. For to whom he has sealed himself in obedience, he is his servant, to whom he obeys, whether of sin or of righteousness. So it is that the devil also has gold and silver and precious stones. it is written to the devil: All the gold of the sea is under him (Job 41:21). And the apostle says that gold and silver vessels are a kind of insult (II Tim. 2:20). when some of them are for honor, as he himself says, "A pot of clay, one thing is fashioned for honor, another for dishonor" (Rom. 9:21). is, from the great and transparent ones he said are unclean. For also in the Apocalypse: The harlot (that is, the body against) is adorned with purple, coconut, and gold, and silver, and precious stones: having an orange cup in her hand, full of curses and filthiness of the whole earth. These are the devil's ornaments, the precious stones: with which he imitates fiery stones, and man has in himself a storehouse of deeds which are more transparent. For where the treasure is, there will also be the heart of man (Matt. 6:21). For of old, man and his earth are one body: since he is also the earth. Whence the apostle does not take things that can be admitted into the body, but he also defined covetousness as being a member of the possessor, saying: Mortify therefore your members which are on the earth, fornication, impurity, passion, evil lust, and covetousness, which is the service of idols. Because of this comes the wrath of God (Col. 3:5, 6). Since when were you created with the Cherubim, I placed you on the holy mountain of God (Ez. 28:14), that is, in Christ, or the Church. for the stones cannot be said to be of another substance, because they have no body. You have departed from sin in your days: from what day were you created, until your iniquities were found in you, by the multitude of your dealings (Ibid., 15). Peter: Behold, you brothers, like living stones, are being built together into spiritual houses (1 Pet. 2:5). And this is how God says to burn the bad brothers: The house of Jacob will be a fire, but the house of Joseph, a flame: but the house of Esau, a stubble. For when a man sins, he is cast down by the demon of God, and he will not be fiery, having lost his Spirit, and will be burned to ashes. but spiritually. For he who does not have a wedding garment is here eternally excluded from the midst of those reclining. Finally, he is sent into darkness, that is, into hardening; until the fire descends forever. For in the world to come, no one will be mixed with the choir of saints, who will be excluded afterwards. Your heart was exalted in your beauty, your knowledge was corrupted in your beauty. a lie: as the Spirit says: When they knew the Lord, they did not magnify the Lord, or gave thanks: but they were vain in their thoughts, saying that they were wise (Rom. 1:22). Because of the multitude of your sins, I threw you to the ground: give yourself up to be dishonored in the sight of kings (Ez. 28:18). If Jeremiah says: "I have brought glory down from heaven to earth." Because of the multitude of your sins, and the iniquity of your trading, your sanctuaries are defiled.] It seems as if he had reproached the chief title, the body of the devil, he says, trading mages, and treasures, spiritual iniquities. And again: Store up for yourselves treasures in heaven (Matt. 6:20). etc. (Ez. 27:12). Again: His business is a holy reward to the Lord (Is. 23:18). And the Apostle: "There is, he says, great business, piety" (I Tim. 6:6). Thus, spiritual wickedness, business it is the treasure of sins, as the Lord says: An evil man, out of the treasure of his heart, casteth forth evil things (Matt. 12:35). And the apostle: Thou hast stored up wrath in the day of wrath (Rom. he does not use the holiness of God rightly, he makes it his own, as God says about his Sabbaths: My soul hates your Sabbaths. The Lord from the Lord, from the Church, as it is written: The sun rose upon the earth, and Lot entered Segor: and the Lord rained upon Sodom and Gomorrah, brimstone and fire from the Lord in heaven (Gen. 19:23). This is the fire that he mentioned above. The house of Jacob, fire: but the house of Esau, the stubble. They will burn in them and eat them: and there will be no fire in the house of Esau and sent Lot out in the midst of the subversion: when God overthrew the cities in which Lot dwelt in them (Gen. 19:29). Did not Lot deserve to be delivered by his own righteousness, as the Scripture would say: God remembered Abraham, and sent Lot out of the midst of the subversion? Or He dwelt in the cities, and not in the city: so that he might say, Cities, where did he live? But it is a prophecy of a future departure. For God remembers the promise to Abraham, when he drove Lot out of all the cities of Sodom, on which the fire will come from the fire of the church, which will be brought out of the midst. And I will give you into ashes in your land, (Ez. 2:18). That is, in men or in the people themselves in their own land, who did not want to be in the land of God. In the sight of men who see you, that is, intelligent people. all who know you among the nations will be grieved over you (Ibid., 19.) For when the Lord strikes or discovers the wicked, those who are wont to be supported by their help are grieved, a weakened part of his body has become Perdition: and you will not be forever.

SEVEN RULES

Necessarium duxi ante omnia quae mihi videntur,libellum Regularum scribere et secretorum leges,veluti claves et luminaria fabricare. Sunt enim quaedamregulae mysticae, quae universae legis recessusobtinent, et veritatis thesauros aliquibus invisibilesfaciunt. Quarum si ratio regularum sine invidia, utcommunicamus, accepta fuerit, clausa quaeque patefient,et obscura dilucidabuntur, ut quis prophetiaeuniversam silvam perambulans, his regulis quodammodolucis tramitibus deductus, ab errore defendatur.Sunt autem regulae istae.I. De Domino et corpore ejus.II. De Domini corpore bipartito.III. De promissis et lege.IV. De specie et genere.V. De temporibus.VI. De recapitulatione.VII. De diabolo et ejus corpore.

LATIN TEXT

Regula I

De Domino et corpore ejus.

Dominum ejusque corpus, id est, Ecclesiam,Scriptura loquitur (II Tim. I, 20), sola ratio discernit:dum quid cuique conveniat, persuadet; sedquia tanta est vis veritatis, extorquet. Alias ullapersona convenitur, quam duplicem esse, diversaduorum officia edocent. Sic per Isaiam: Hic, inquit,peccata nostra fert, et pro nobis dolet, et ipsevulneratus est propter facinora nostra. Deus traditillum pro peccatis nostris, etc. (Isa. LIII, 4, 6, sec.LXX), quae in Dominum convenire omnis Ecclesiaeore celebratur. Sequitur autem et dicit de eodem:Et Deus vult eum purgare a plaga, et vult Deus a doloreauferre illi lucem, et formare illum prudentia(Ibid., 10, 11). Numquid ei, quem tradidit pro peccatisnostris, vult ostendere lucem, et eum formareprudentia, cum ipse sit lux et sapientia Dei? et noncorpori ejus? Quare manifestum est, sola ratione videriposse quando a capite ad corpus transitum faciat.Daniel quoque lapidem de monte praecisumimpegisse in corpus regnorum mundi, et in pulveremcomminuisse Dominum dicit. Montem vero effectum,et implevisse universam terram corpus ejus.Non enim sicut quidam dicunt, in contumeliam regniDei, invictaeque haereditatis Christi, quod nonsine dolore dico. Dominus totum mundum potestate(Matth. XXVIII, 18), et non sui corporis plenitudineoccupavit. Dicunt enim eo monte mundum impletum;quod liceat Christiano in omni loco, quodantea non nisi in Sion licebat, offerre. Quod si itaest, non opus erat dicere, ex lapide montem effectum,et incrementis mundum coepisse. Dominusenim noster Christus, ante mundi constitutionem(Joan. XVII, 2), hanc habuit claritatem, et cum homoille, Dei filius fuerit, non paulatim, ut lapis,sed uno tempore accepit omnem [23] pietatem in coeloet in terra. Lapis autem incrementis factus estmons, et crescendo terram omnem texit. Quod sipotestate implesset universam terram, non corpore,lapidi non compararetur. Potestas enim res est impalpabilis,lapis vero corpus palpabile. Nec sola rationemonstratur corpus, non caput crescere: sedetiam Apostolica auctoritate firmatur: Crescatis,inquit, per omnia in eum, qui est caput Christus, exquo omne corpus constructum et connexum, per omnemtactum subministrationis in mensuram uniuscujusquepartis, incrementum corporis facit, in aedificationemsui (Ephes. IV, 15, 16). Et iterum: Non tenetiscaput, ex quo omne corpus per tactum et conjunctioneconstructum et subministratum, crescit in incrementumDei

(Coloss. II, 29). Non ergo caput quod exorigine idem est, sed corpus crescit ex capite. Adpropositum redeamus. Scriptum est de Domino etejus corpore; quid cui conveniat, ratione discernendum:Angelis suis mandavit de te, ut custodiantte in omnibus viis tuis: in manibus ferent te, ne offendasad lapidem pedem tuum. Super aspidem et basiliscumambulabis, et conculcabis leonem, et draconem.Quoniam in me speravit, eripiam eum, protegameum, quoniam cognovit nomen meum. Invocavit me,et ego exaudiam eum, cum eo sum in tribulatione,eripiam eum et glorificabo eum. Longitudine dierumadimplebo eum, et ostendam illi salutare meum(Psal. XC, 11-16). Numquid de cujus obsequiomandavit angelis suis Deus, eidem ostendit salutaresuum, et non corpori ejus? Iterum: Sicut sponsoimposuit mihi mitram, et sicut sponsam ornavit me ornatu(Isa. LXI, 10, sec. LXX). Unum corpus dixitutriusque sexus sponsi et sponsae: sed quid in Dominum,quid in Ecclesiam conveniat, ratione cognoscitur.Et idem Dominus dicit in Apocalypsi: Egosum sponsus et sponsa (Apoc. XVIII, 23). Et iterum:Exierunt obviam sponso et sponsae (Matth. XXV, 1).Et iterum, quid capiti et corpori, ratione discernendumsit per Isaiam declaratur: Sic dicit Dominus[24]ut exaudiant eum gentes (Isa. XLV, 1-3). Sequitur etdicit, quod non nisi corpori conveniat: Et dabo tibithesauros absconditos et invisibiles aperiam tibi, utscias quoniam ego sum Dominus, qui voco nomentuum, Deus Israel, propter Jacob puerum meum, etIsrael electum meum. Propter testamentum enim quoddisposuit Patribus, ad agnoscendum se, Deus aperitcorpori Christi thesauros invisibiles, quos oculus nonvidit, nec auris audivit, nec illi in cor hominis ascenderunt(I Cor. II, 9), sed nec [25] obturati hominis, quinon est in corpore Christi: Ecclesiae autem revelavitDeus per Spiritum sanctum ista quidem, quamvishoc gratiae Dei sit. Adhibita tamen ratione, aliquandofacilius videntur. Sunt alia in quibus hujusmodiratio minus claret; eo quod, sive in Domino,sive in corpore ejus recta conveniat dictum. Quamobremsola et majore Dei gratia videri possunt. Sicin Evangelio: Amodo, inquit, videbitis filium hominissedentem ad dextram virtutis Dei, et venientemin nubibus coeli (Matth. XXVI, 64). Alio loco dicit:Non visuros venientem in nubibus coeli, nisi novissimotantum die plangentes omnes tribus terrae. Et tuncvidebunt filium hominis venientem in nubibus coeli(Matth. XXIV, 30). Utrumque autem fieri necesse est.Sed primo corporis est adventus, id est Ecclesiaejugiter venientis in eadem claritate invisibili; deindecapitis, id est, Domini in manifesta claritate. Si enimdiceret: Amodo videbitis venientem, solius corporisintelligendus esset adventus. Si autem videbitis,capitis adventus. Nunc vero amodo, inquit, videbitisvenientem, quoniam corpore suo jugiter venitnativitate et similium passionum claritate. Sienim renati Christi membra efficiuntur, et membraquae corpus efficiunt, Christus est qui venit, quoniamnativitas adventus est sicut scriptum est: Illuminatomnem hominem venientem in hunc mundum(Joan. I, 9). Et iterum: Generatio vadit, et generatiovenit (Eccle. I, 4). Et iterum: Sicut audistis, quiaAntichristus venit (I Joan. II, 18). Iterum de eodemcorpore: Si enim iste qui venit, alium Christum praedicat(II Cor. XI, 4). Unde Dominus, cum de signoadventus sui interrogaretur, de illo adventu suo coepitdisputare, qui ab inimico corpore signis et prodigiisimitari potest: Cavete, inquit, ne quis vos seducat(Matth. XXIV, 4). Multi venient, in nomine meo,id est in nomine corporis mei. Novissimo autem adventuDomini, id est, consummationis totius adventusejus, nemo, ut aliqui putant, moreretur. Sedquo plenius ista dicantur, ordini suo relinquamus.Nec illud erit absurdum, quod ex uno totum corpusvolumus intelligi, ut Filium hominis Ecclesiam, quoniamEcclesia, id est Filii Dei redacti in unum corpus,dicti sunt Filius Dei, dictus unus homo, dictietiam Deus, sicut per Apostolum: Super omnequod dicitur Deus, aut quod colitur (II Thess. II, 4).Qui dicitur Deus, Ecclesia est. Quod autem colitur,Deus summus est: ut in templo Dei sedeat, ostendensse, quod ipse sit Deus, id est, quod ipse sit Ecclesia.Quasi diceret: In templo Dei sedeat, ostendens sequod ipse sit Dei templum. Aut in Deo sedeat, ostendensse, quod ipse sit Deus. Sed hunc intellectumnon minus, ut novimus, voluit obscurare Daniel derege novissimo: In Dominum, inquit, locus ejus glorificabitur(Dan. XI, 38, sec. LXX): id est clarificabitur,velut Ecclesiam in loco Ecclesiae, in loco sancto,abominatione vastationis, in Deum, id est, inEcclesiam subornavit. Et Dominus totum populum,sponsam dicit et sororem. Et Apostolus Virginemsanctam, et adversum corpus, hominem peccati. EtDavid totam, Christum, Ecclesiam dicit: Faciensmisericordias Christo suo David, et semini ejus usquein saeculum (Psal. XVII, 51). Et apostolus Paulus,corpus Christi, Christum appellat: Sicut enim unumcorpus est, membra autem habet multa; omnia autemmembra ex uno corpore, cum sint multa, unum corpussunt: sic et Christus (I Cor. XII, 12), id est Christicorpus, quod est Ecclesia. Iterum: Gaudeo inpassionibus pro vobis: et repleo, quae desunt pressurarumChristi (Coloss. I, 24), id est, Ecclesiae. Nihilenim defuit Christi passionibus: quoniam sufficitdiscipulo, ut sit sicut magister ejus. Sic ergo adventumChristi pro locis accipiemus. Item in Exodo,omnes filios Dei, unum filium, et omnes primogenitosAegyptiorum, primogenitum esse, sic Deo dicente,cognoscimus: Haec dices, inquit, Pharaoni:Haec dicit Dominus: Filius meus primogenitus Israel.Dixi tibi:

Dimitte populum meum, ut serviat mihi. Tuautem noluisti dimittere eum (Exod. IV, 22). Undeergo: Ecce ego occidam filium tuum primogenitum.Et David, vineam Domini, unum filium, sic ait:Deus virtutum, convertere: respice de coelo, et vide, etvisita vineam istam, et perfice eam, quam plantavitdextera tua, et super filium hominis, quem confirmastitibi (Psal. LXXIX, 15). Et Apostolus filium Dei dicit,qui filio Dei mixtus est: Paulus servus Jesu Christi,vocatus Apostolus, segregatus in Evangelium Dei, quodante promiserat per prophetas suos, in scripturis sanctisde filio suo, qui factus est ei, ex semine David secundumcarnem. Qui praedestinatus est filius Dei invirtute, secundum Spiritum sanctificationis ex resurrectionemortuorum Jesu Christi Domini nostri (Rom.I, 1-4). Si diceret de filio suo, ut ex resurrectionemortuorum, unum filium ostenderet; nunc autem,de filio, inquit, suo, ex resurrectione mortuorum JesuChristi Domini nostri. Sed qui factus sit filius Dei exresurrectione Christi, apertius ostendit de filio suo,quia factus est ei, ex semine David secundum carnem,qui praedestinatus est filius Dei. Dominus etenimnoster, non est praedestinatus filius Dei, quiaDeus est, et coaequalis est Patri, qui ex quo creatusest, hoc est. Sed ille, cui secundum Lucam dicit inbaptismo: Filius meus es tu, ego hodie genui te(Psal. II, 7). Qui ex semine David, mixtus est principaliSpiritui, et factus est ipse filius Dei, ex resurrectioneDomini nostri Jesu Christi: id est, dum resurgitin Christo semen David: non ille, de quo aitipse David: Sic dicit Dominus Domino meo (Psal.CIX, 1). Itaque facti sunt duo, una caro, Verbum carofactum est (Joan. I, 14), et caro Deus: quia non exsanguine, sed ex Deo nati sumus. Apostolus dicit:Erunt duo in carne una. Sacramentum hoc magnumest: ego autem dico, in Christo et in Ecclesia (Ephes.V, 31, 32). Unum namque semen promisit DeusAbrahae; ut quanticumque Christi miscerentur, unusesset in Christo, sicut Apostolus dicit: Omnes vos,unum estis in Christo Jesu. Si autem vos unum estis inChristo Jesu: ergo Abrahae semen estis, et secundumpromissionem haeredes (Gal. III, 28, 29).Distat autem, inter unum estis: et unus estis. Quotiescumquealter alteri voluntate misceatur uni, unumsunt. Sicut Dominus dicit: Ego et Pater, unum sumus(Joan. X, 3). Quotiescumque autem et corporalitermiscentur, et in unam carnem duo solidantur:unum sunt corpus. Itaque in capite suo filius estDei; et Deus in corpore suo, filius est hominis, quiquotidie nascendo venit, et crescit in templum sanctumDei. Templum enim bipartitum est. Cujus parsaltera, quamvis lapidibus magnis exstruatur, destruitur:neque in eo lapis super lapidem relinquetur.Istius nobis jugis adventus cavendus est, donecde medio ejus discedat Ecclesia.

Regula II

De Domini corpore bipartito.

Regula bipartiti corporis Domini multo necessarioret a nobis tanto diligentius perspicienda, et peromnes Scripturas ante oculos habenda est. Sicutenim, ut supra dictum est, a capite ad corpus rationesola videtur: ita a parte corporis ad partem, adextra ad sinistram, vel a sinistra ad dextram reditusin supradicto capite claret. Dum enim dicit uni corpori:Thesauros aperiam tibi invisibiles, ut scias, quoniamego sum Deus, et assumam te (Isa. XLV, 3): et adjecit:Tu autem me non cognovisti, quoniam ego sumDeus, et non est alius absque me Deus, et nesciebas me(Ibid., 4, 5). Numquid, licet unum corpus alloquitur,in unam mentem convenit, thesauros invisibiles aperiamtibi, ut cognoscas, quoniam ego sum Deus, propterpuerum meum Jacob: Et tu autem me non cognovisti?In eadem: et non accepit Jacob, quod Deus promisit.Aut in unam mentem non convenit: Tu autem menon cognovisti, et nesciebas me: Nesciebas enim non dicitur,nisi ei, qui jam scit. Non cognovisti autem illidicitur, qui licet ad hoc vocatus sit, ut cognosceret,et ejusdem corporis sit visibiliter, et Deo labiis quidemappropinquet; corde tamen separatus sit. Huicdicit, tu autem me non cognovisti. Iterum: Ducam caecosin viam, quam non noverunt, et semitas quas non cognoverunt,calcabunt: et faciam illis tenebras in lucem,et prava in directum. Haec verba faciam, et non derelinquameos. Ipse autem conversi sunt retro (Isa. XLII,16, 17). Numquid, quos dixit non derelinquam, iidemconversi sunt retro, et non pars eorum? Iterum dicitDominus ad Jacob: Noli timere, quia tecum sum.Ab Oriente adducam semen tuum, et ab Occidente colligamte. Dicam Aquiloni, da; et Africo, noli vetare.Adduc filios meos de terra longinqua, et filias meas asummo terrae, et omnes in quibus vocatum est nomenmeum. In gloriam enim meam paravi illum, et finxiillum, et produxi plebem caecam, et oculi eorum suntsimiliter caeci, et surdas aures habent (Isa. XLIII, 5, 8).Numquid, quos in gloriam suam paravit, iidem suntcaeci et surdi? Iterum: Patres tui primo; principeseorum facinus admiserunt in me, et inquinaverunt principestui sancta mea, et dedi perire Jacob, et Israel inmaledictum (Ibid. 25). Nunc audi me, puer meus Jacob,et Israel quem elegi (Isa. XLIV, 1). Ostendit illi Jacobdedisse perire, et Israel in maledictum, quem nonelegerat. Iterum: Finxi te puerum meum, meus es tu,Israel, noli oblivisci mei. Ecce enim delevi velut nubemfacinora tua, et sicut nimbum peccata tua. Converteread me, et redimam te (Ibid., 21). Numquid, cujuspeccata delevit, cui dicit, meus es tu: Et, ne obliviscatursui: commemorat eidem, et dicit, converteread me, aut alicujus antequam convertatur, peccatadelentur? Iterum: Scio quoniam reprobatusreprobaberis: propter nomen tuum, ostendum tibidignitatem meam, et praeclara mea superducam tibi(Isa. XLVIII, 8, 9). Numquid reprobato ostenditdignitatem suam, et praeclara sua inducit ei? Iterum:Non [26] senior, non Angelus: sed ipse consideravit eospropter quod diligeret eos, et parceret illis. Ipse redemitillos, et assumpsit illos, et exaltavit illos omnes diessaeculi. Ipsi autem contumaces fuerunt et exacerbaveruntSpiritum sanctum (Isa. LXIII, 9, 10, sec. LXX).Quos omnes dies saeculi exaltavit, quo tempore fueruntcontumaces, aut exacerbaverunt Spiritum sanctum?Iterum aperte Deus uni corpori firmitatem,et interitum promittit, dicens: Hierusalem civitas dives,tabernacula quae non commovebuntur, neque agitabunturpali tabernaculi tui in aeternum tempus, nequefunes ejus rumpentur (Isa. XXXIII, 20, 21, sec. LXX).Et adjecit: rupti sunt funes tui, quia non valuit arbornavis tuae, inclinaverunt tua vela et non tollet signum,donec tradatur in perditionem (Ibid. 23). Iterum ostenditbreviter bipartitum Christi corpus: Fusca sumet decora (Cant. 1, 4). Absit enim, ut Ecclesia, quaenon habet maculam, aut rugam (Ephes. V, 27), quamDominus suo sanguine mundavit, aliqua ex parte fuscasit, nisi in parte sinistra, per quam nomen Dei blasphematurin gentibus; alias, tota speciosa est, sicutdicit. Tota speciosa es, proxima mea: et reprehensionulla est in te (Cant. IV, 7). Etenim dicit qua de causasit fusca et speciosa: ut tabernacula Cedar, et pelles Salomonis.Duo tabernacula ostendit: Regium et servile.Utrumque tamen semen Abrahae. Cedar enim filius estIsmael. Alio denique loco, cum isto Cedar, id est,cum servo ex Abraham, diuturnam mansionem sicingemuit Ecclesia dicens: Heu me! quia peregrinatiomea longinqua facta est: Habitavi cum tabernaculis Cedar,multum peregrinata est anima mea. Cum odientibuspacem, eram pacificus: cum loquerer illis, debellabantme gratis (Psal. CXIX, 5-7, sec. LXX). Nonpossum autem dicere, tabernaculum Cedar, praeterEcclesiam esse. Ipse enim dicit: Tabernaculum Cedaret Salomonis: Unde fusca sum, inquit, et decora.Non enim Ecclesia in his qui foris sunt, fusca est.Hoc mysterio Dominus in Apocalypsi septem angelosdicit, id est, Ecclesiam septiformem, nunc sanctoset praeceptorum custodes: nunc eosdem et multorumcriminum reos, et poenitentia dignos ostendit.Et in Evangelio unum praepositorum corpus, diversimeriti manifestat, dicens: Beatus ille servus, quemadveniens dominus illius, invenerit ita facientem (Luc.XII, 43.) Et de eodem: si autem nequam ille servus,quem Dominus dividit in duas partes (Luc. XIX, 21).Dico: numquid omnem dividet, aut findet? Denique totumnon totum: sed partem ejus cum hypocritis ponet(Matth. XXIV, 51). In uno enim corpus ostendit. Hocitaque corpus accipiendum est per omnes scripturas,sicubi Deus dicit, ob meritum Israel periturum, authaereditatem suam exsecrabilem. Apostolus enim copioseita disputat, maxime ad Romanos, in parteaccipiendum, quidquid de toto corpore dictum est.Ad Israel, inquit, dicit: Tota die expandi manus measad plebem contradicentem (Rom. X, 21). Et ut ostenderetde parte dictum: Dico, inquit, Numquid repulitDeus plebem suam? Absit. Nam et ego Israelita sum exsemine Abrahae, tribu Benjamin. Non repulit Deus plebemsuam, quam praescivit (Rom. XI, 1, 2). Et postquamdocuit, quemadmodum haec locutio intelligendaesset; eodem genere locutionis ostendit,unum corpus et bonum esse et malum, dicens:Secundum Evangelium quidem inimici propter vos: secundumelectionem autem, dilecti propter patres (Ib. 28).Numquid idem dilecti, qui inimici, aut potest in causautrumque convenire? Ita Dominus in omnibus Scripturis.Unum corpus seminis Abrahae in omnibusgentibus crescere et florere atque perire testatur.

Regula III

De promissis et Lege.

Exponitur Paulus ad Rom. et ad Gal., et Isai. c. XLVIII. Auctoritas divina est, neminem aliquando ex operibuslegis justificari potuisse. Eadem auctoritate firmissimumest, non defuisse, qui legem facerent,et justificarentur. Scriptum est: Quaecumque lex loquitur, his dicitqui in lege sunt: ut omne os obstruatur, et subjectusfiat omnis mundus Deo. Quia non justificatur ex legeomnis caro in conspectu ejus. Per legem enim agnitiopeccati (Rom. III, 19, 20). Iterum: Peccatum vestrinon dominabitur. Non enim estis sub lege (Rom. VI, 4).Iterum: Et nos in Christum credimus: ut justificemurex fide, et non ex operibus legis (Gal. II, 16). Iterum:Si enim data esset lex, quae posset vivificare, omnimodoex lege esset justitia. Sed conclusit Scripturaomnia sub peccato: ut promissio ex fide Jesu Christi dareturcredentibus (Gal. III, 21, 22). Sed dicet quis: aChristo, et infra non justificat lex, suo tamen temporejustificavit. Huic occurrit auctoritas apostoli Petri,qui, cum gentes a fratribus cogerentur sub jugo legis,sic ait: Quid tentatis Dominum imponere volentesjugum super collum discentium, quod neque patresnostri, neque nos potuimus portare (Act. XV, 10). Etapostolus Paulus: Cum essemus, inquit, in carne,passiones peccatorum quae per legem sunt, operabanturin membris nostris, ut fructum afferrent morti (Rom.VII, 5). Et contra, idem Apostolus dicit: Justitia,quae ex lege est, conservatus sine querela (Philipp. III,6). Quod si tanti Apostoli auctoritas deesset: quiddici potuit contra testimonium Domini dicentis: Ecce!vere Israelita in quo dolus non est (Joan. I, 47).Quod et si Dominus hoc testimonium non dignareturperhibere: quis tam sacrilegus, quis tam tumorestuporis elatus diceret, Moysen et Prophetas, velomnes Sanctos justitiam non fecisse, aut justificatosnon esse? cum Scriptura dicat de Zacharia etuxore ejus: Erant justi ambo in conspectu Dei, ambulantesin omnibus mandatis et justificationibus Dei sinequerela (Luc. I, 6). Et Dominus non venerit vocarejustos, sed peccatores (Matth. IX, 13). Lex autem,quomodo justificari potuit a peccato, quae ad hocdata est: Lex autem subintravit, ut multiplicareturpeccatum (Rom. V, 20). Illud autem scire debemuset tenere: numquam omnino interceptum esse semenAbrahae, ab Isaac usque ad hodiernum. Semenautem Abrahae non carnale, sed spirituale, quod nonex lege est, sed ex repromissione est. Alterum enimsemen carnale est, quod ex lege est a monte Sina,Quod est Agar in servitute generans. Ille quidem, quiex ancilla carnaliter natus est. Qui autem ex libera,ex promissione (Gal. IV, 23, 24). Non esse autem semenAbrahae, nisi quod ex fide est, Apostolus dicit:Cognoscitis ergo, quoniam qui ex fide sunt, hi sunt filiiAbrahae (Gal. III, 7)? Et iterum: Vos autem, fratressecundum Isaac, promissionis filii estis (Gal. IV, 28).Semen ergo Abrahae, non ex lege, sed ex promissioneest, quod ex Isaac jugiter transit. Si autemconstat semen Abrahae, quod ex fide est, constat,quia numquam fuit ex lege. Non enim potuitex lege esse, et ex fide. Lex enim et fides, diversares est. Quia lex non est fidei, sed operum. Sicutscriptum est: Lex non est ex fide, sed qui fecerit ea,vivet in eis (Gal. III, 12). Abraham ergo fide semperfilios habuit, lege numquam. Non enim ex lege promissioest Abrahae, aut semini ejus, ut haeres essetmundi, sed per justitiam fidei. Si enim qui per legemipsi sunt haeredes, vacua est fides, et vacua estpromissio. Lex enim iram operatur. Si ergo nec fides,nec promissio Abrahae destrui potest, ab ortusui jugiter mansit. Nec, data lege, impedita est:quominus Abrahae filii secundum promissionem fideigenerentur. Dicit enim Apostolus, post quadringentoset triginta annos datam legem non obfuisse, necdestruxisse promissionem: Si enim ex lege [27], jamnon ex promissione. Abrahae autem, per repromissionemdonavit Deus

(Ibid., 18). Et alio loco: Lex ergoadversus promissa Dei? Absit (Ibid., 21). Videmus legemad promissa non pertinere, nec aliquando alteramin alteram impegisse, sed utramque ordinemsuum tenuisse. Quia sicut lex numquam fidei obfuit,ita nec fides legem destruxit. Sicut scriptum est: Legemergo destruimus per fidem? absit, sed legem statuimus(Rom. III, 31), id est, firmamus: invicem namquefirmant. Ergo filii Abrahae non ex lege sunt, sed exfide per repromissionem. Quaerendum autem quemadmodumhi, qui ex operibus legis neganturpotuisse justificari, in lege positi, et legem operantes,justificati fuerint. Quaerendum praeterea,cur post promissionem fidei, quae nullo modo destruipotest, data est lex, quae non est ex fide: excujus operibus nemo justificaretur, quia, Quotquotex operibus legis sunt, sub maledicto sunt. Scriptumest enim: Maledictus qui non permanserit in omnibus,quae scripta sunt in libro legis, ut faciat ea(Gal. III, 10). Apostolus denique huic quaestioniprospiciens, cum asserat omnimodo filios Abrahaedono Dei semper fuisse per fidem, non per legem factorum,ex alterius persona respondit sibi, dicens:Quid ergo lex factorum (Rom. III, 27)? Id est: Siex fide filii, cur data est lex factorum, cum sufficeretpromissio generandis filiis Abrahae, et fide essentnutriendi? Quia justus ex fide vivit (Rom. I, 17;Gal. III, 11; Heb. X, 30). Antequam enim se interrogasset:Quid ergo lex factorum? jam dixerat, utviverent, qui ex fide justificari non possent, hocmodo: Quoniam autem ex lege nemo justificatur apudDeum: justus autem ex fide vivit (Gal. III, 11). Ostenditpraeterea, dictum esse per Prophetam, Exfide vivit: ut manifestum fieret, quemadmodum viverent,qui legem facere non possent. Sed minuslucet, quid sit: Justus ex fide vivit (Habac. II, 4).Non enim potuit quisquam justus in lege positus vivere,nisi opera legis fecisset, et omnia opera: sinminus, maledictus esset. Dedit Deus legem, et dixit:Non concupisces (Exod. XX, 17; Deut. V, 21). Statimoccasione accepta, peccatum, per mandatum operatumest omnem concupiscentiam. Necesse est enimpassiones peccatorum, quae per legem sunt, operariin membris ejus, qui in lege est. Propterea ea data est:ut abundaret peccatum (Rom. V, 20), quia virtus peccati,lex. Venundatus autem sub peccato, jam non quodvult operatur bonum, sed quod non vult malum:consentit enim legi, secundum interiorem hominem.Expugnatur autem aliter lege membrorum, trahiturquecaptivus, neque aliquando liberari potuit, nisisola gratia per fidem. Est autem magnum crimenperfidiae, non attendisse genus armorum, quibusviolentia peccati expugnaretur, et e contra, magnificaefidei est inquisisse et vidisse. Est ergo sacrilegamens, et male de Deo sentiens, quae cum legemnullo modo humanitus posse fieri, et ad ulciscendumparatam videret; non intellexerit esse aliquodremedium vitae: nec fieri potuisse, ut bonus Deus,qui sciebat legem non potuisse fieri, alterum vitaeaditum non reliquisset: et adversum homines, quosad vitam fecerat, undiqueversum vitae vias clausisset.Hoc fides non tulit, non admisit. Sed cuminfirmitate carnis, et virtute peccati urgeretur:Deus dedit claritatem. Sciens Dominum bonum etjustum, et viscera suae miserationis contra operamanuum suarum non clausisse: intellexit esse iterad vitam, et faciendae legis remedium vidit. Deusenim cum diceret: Non concupisces; non denudavit,quemadmodum id provenire posset, sed vere atquedecise dixit: Non concupisces; quoniam id reperiendumreliquit. Si enim mandaret a se proventumpostulari, legem destruxerat et fidem. Ut quid enimlegem daret, si legem in omnibus factorum polliceretur?Aut quid fidei relinqueretur, si fidem, auxiliumpollicendo, praeveniret? Nunc autem bono fideidedit legem, ministram mortis: ut amatores vitae,fide vitam viderent, et justi, fide viverent, qui opuslegis non ex sua virtute, sed ex Dei dono fieri possecrederent. Lex enim a carne fieri non potest: quaecum facta non fuerit, punit. Quae ergo spes hominifaciendae legis, et fugiendae mortis: nisi opis et misericordiaeDei, quam fides invenit? Caro legi Deisubjecta non est; neque enim potest. Qui autem incarne sunt, Deo placere non possunt. Vos autem nonestis in carne, sed in spiritu; siquidem Spiritus Deiin vobis est. Si quis autem Spiritum Christi non habet,hic non est ejus (Rom. VIII, 7, 9). Ostendit SpiritumDei et Christi, idem esse. Ostendit praeterea,qui Spiritum Dei habuerit, in carne non esse. Siergo unus est Spiritus Dei et Christi; prophetae etsancti quia Spiritum Dei habuerunt, Spiritum Christihabuerunt. Si spiritum Dei habuerunt, in carnenon fuerunt, et legem fecerunt: quia caro est inimicain Deum, et legi ejus subjecta non est. Quiergo ad Deum confugit, accepit Spiritum Dei, quoaccepto, mortificata est caro; qua mortificata, potuitfacere legem spiritualis, liberatus a lege, quiajusto non est posita. Et iterum: Si Spiritu Dei agimini,non estis sub lege (Gal. V, 18). Qua re manifestum,quia patres nostri, qui Spiritum Dei habuerunt,non fuerunt sub lege. Quamdiu enim quis in carneest, id est, Spiritum Dei non habet, dominatur eilex. Si autem tradiderit se gratiae, moritur legi, etfacit in illo legem spiritus, mortua carne, quae legiDei subjecta esse non potest. Quod enim gerebatur,id etiam nunc geritur, non enim quia sub lege nonsumus, cessavit interdictio illa concupiscentiae, etnon magis aucta est; sed nos in revelatam gratiamconcurrimus per fidem, edocti a Domino, opus legisde ejus misericordia postulare et dicere: Fiat voluntastua: Et, Libera nos a malo (Matth. VI, 10, 13).Illi autem in non revelatam per eamdem fidemcoacti metu mortis, quam ministra lege parato gladiointentari videbant. Lex data est, donec veniret semen,cui promissum est et evangelizare fidem. Anteavero, lex cogebat in fide; quasi sine lege non possitexprimi fides, ad exquirendam Dei gratiam, eo quodpeccatum virtutem non haberet. Data vero lege,passiones quae per legem sunt, operabantur in membrisnostris, urgentes in peccatum, ut vel necessitate,urgerentur in fide, quae imploraret gratiamDei in auxilio tolerantiae. Custodiam carceris passiusumus, lege minante mortem, et undiqueversuminsuperabili muro ambientem, cujus ambitus solauna janua fuit gratia. Huic januae custos, fides praesidebat:ut nemo illum carcerem effugeret, nisi cuifides aperuisset; et qui hanc januam non pulsaret,intra septa legis moreretur. Legem paedagogum passiusumus, qui nos cogeret studere fidei, qui nos cogeretin Christo. Dicit enim Apostolus, propterea datamlegem, ut nos custodia sua concluderet in fidem,quantum futurum erat revelari in Christo, qui estfinis legis, quo vixerunt omnes, qui fidem gratiaeDei exquisierunt. Prius, inquit, quam veniret fides,sub lege custodiebamur, conclusi in fidem, quamfuturum erat revelari. Lex itaque paedagogus nosterfuit in Christo (Gal. III, 24): ut ex fide justificemur.Lex, inquam, [28] fides erat demonstratrix. Sed dicetquis: si in utilitate fidei data est lex, cur non aborigine seminis Abrahae, siquidem juge fuit? Revera,juge fuit. Jugis et fides, ut genitrix filiorumAbrahae. Jugis et lex, per dignoscentiamboni et mali. Sed post promissionem filiorumAbrahae, multiplicatis eis secundum carnem, multiplicandumerat et semen Abrahae, quod non est exfide. Quae multiplicatio, evenire non possit sine adjutoriolegis multiplicatae, et multitudo in fidemnecdum revelatam, sicut jam dictum est, vel necessitatedeuceretur. Providentia itaque Dei, sanctumex augendo gubernandoque semen Abrahae, ut severitateet metu legis, multi compellerentur in fidem,et semen fulciretur usque ad fidei revelationem:Lex autem subintravit, ut multiplicaretur peccatum.Ubi, inquit, multiplicatum est peccatum, superabundavitgratia (Rom. V, 20). Non dixit, nata, sed superabundavit.Ab initio enim data est fugientibuslegis molestias atque dominium. Abundavit autemmultiplicata lege, superabundavit vero in omnemcarnem, revelata in Christum. Qui veniens restaurare,quae in coelo, et quae in terra, evangelizavit fidemhis, qui proxime et qui longe (Is. LVII, 19; Ephes.II, 17), id est, peccatoribus Israel et gentibus. Justienim Israel ex fide, in eamdem fidem vocati sunt.Idem namque spiritus, eadem fides, eadem gratiaper Christum semper data est. Quorum plenitudinemveniens, remoto legis velamine, omni gentilargitus est, quae modo, non genere a futuris differebant.Aliter enim numquam fuit semen Abrahae.Quod si quisquam praeter fidem justificatus est: filiusAbrahae non fuit. Quoniam filius Abrahae dici nonpotest, si ex lege, et non sicut Abraham, ex fidejustificatus est. Ab eadem namque imagine gratiaeet spiritus, in eamdem transisse Ecclesiam, docetApostolus, dicens: Nos autem omnes, revelata faciegloriam Dei speculantes, in eamdem imaginem commutamur,a claritate in claritatem (II Cor. III, 18). Dicitet ante passionem Domini gloriam fuisse, et negatex lege excludi, id est, exprimi, produci, effici potuisse.Unde, manifestum est, ex fide fuisse. Ubiergo, inquit, gloriatio? Exclusa est. Per quam legem?Et numquid operum? Non; sed per legem fidei (Rom.III, 27, 28). Quid enim Scriptura dicit? CrediditAbraham Deo, et reputatum est ei in justitiam (Rom.IV, 3). Ad gloriam ex eadem gloria transivimus:quae non fuit ex lege. Si ex operibus fuit, habetgloriam, sed non ad Deum. Etenim impossibile est,sine gratia Dei, habere aliquam gloriam. Una estenim gloria, et uno genere semper fuit. Nemo enimvicit, nisi cui Deus vicerit, quod non est ex lege:sed qui fecerit. In fidem autem, Deus infirmum facitadversarium nostrum. Propterea, qui gloriatur, inDomino glorietur (I Cor. I, 31). Si enim quod vincimus,nostrum non est: non est ex operibus, sed exfide. Nihil est igitur quod ex nobis gloriemur. Nihilenim habemus, quod non accepimus. Si sumus, exDeo sumus: ut magnitudo virtutis sit Dei, et nonex nobis. Omne opus nostrum, fides est. Quae quantafuerit, tantum Deus operatur in nobis. Cum in hocgloriatur Salomon fuisse non ex homine; sed exDei dono esse hominis continentia: Cum scivi, inquit,quia aliter non possum esse continens, nisi Deusdederit. Et hoc ipsum erat sapientiae, scire, cujus hocdonum esset, Adii Dominum, et deprecatus sum (Sap.VIII, 21). Judicio Salomonis credendum est, non exoperibus, sed ex gratia Dei, omnes justificatos, quiscierunt opus legis a Deo implendum, quo possintgloriari. Dicit autem Apostolus: Ut omnis caro nonglorietur in conspectu Dei (I Cor. I, 29). Mali omnimodo,quod Deum non cognoverunt: justi, quodnon suum, sed Dei sint opus. Inutilia, inquit, et abjectaelegit Deus, quae non sunt: ut ea, quae sunt,evacuarentur, ut non glorietur in conspectu Dei omniscaro. Ex ipso autem vos estis in Christo Jesu, qui factusest vobis sapientia a Deo, et justitia, et sanctimonia,et redemptio: ut secundum quod scriptum est: Quigloriatur, in Domino glorietur (Ibid., 28-30). Et iterum:Gratia estis salvati per fidem, et hoc non ex vobis(Ephes. II, 8). Dei donum est, non ex operibus,ne forte quis glorietur: ipsius enim sumus figmentum,creati in Christo. Sic nulla caro aliquando exlege, id est ex operibus justificari potest, ut omnisjustus ex Deo gloriam haberet. Est aliud, quodnemo glorietur in conspectu Dei: Deus enim sicsuis operatur, ut sit quod et dimittat:

Nemo estenim mundus a sorde, nec si unius diei sit vita ejus(Job. XIV, 4). Et David dicit: Non introeas in judiciumcum servo tuo, quoniam non justificabitur inconspectu tuo omnis vivens (Ps. CXLII, 2). Et Salomonin dedicatione templi: Non est, inquit, homo qui nonpeccavit (III Reg. VIII, 46). Et iterum: Tibi soli deliqui(Ps. L, 6). Quis enim gloriabitur castum se haberecor? Aut quis gloriabitur, mundum esse apeccato? Parum fuit de corde casto, id est, a cogitationibus,nisi et a peccato se mundum nemo gloriaretur.Omnis victoria non ex operibus, sed Deimiseratione conceditur, sicut scriptum est: Qui tecoronat in miseratione et misericordia (Ps. CIV, 4). Etmater martyrum filio suo sic dicit: Ut illa miserationecum fratribus tuis te recipiam (II Machab. VII,29). Justi autem perfecerunt voluntatem Dei votoatque conatu, qui nituntur et concupiscunt Deo servire,non tamen in lege. Quae si justificasset, omnesjusti unius essent meriti, quia parem de omnibusexigit observationem: sin minus, operaretur maledictio:si autem disparis erat meriti, quis quantumcredidit sibi dari, tantum gratiae Dei miserentisaccepit, transformatus a gloria in gloriam, sicut aDei spiritu, id est, ex eodem in eumdem? Tale estenim, quia post Christum fides data est: quale,quia Spiritus sanctus, cum semper omnes prophetaeet justi eodem spiritu vixerunt. Non enim aliter viverepotuerunt, quam spiritu fidei. Quotquot enimsub lege fuerunt, occisi sunt. Quia littera occidit,spiritus autem vivificat (II Cor. III, 6). Et tamen dicitDominus de eodem Spiritu: Nisi ego abiero, ille nonveniet (Joan. XVI, 7), cum et Apostolis jam dedisseteumdem spiritum. Apostolus autem dicit, eumdemspiritum apud antiquos fuisse: Habentes autem eumdemspiritum fidei, sicut scriptum est: Credidi propterquod locutus sum (II Cor. IV, 13). Eumdem spiritumfidei, dixit habuisse eumdem, qui dixit: Credidipropter quod locutus sum (Ps. CXV, 1): et id confirmat,dicens: Et nos credimus; ideoque et loquimur. Dicendo:Et nos, ostendit et illos eodem spiritu fidei credidisse.Unde manifestum est, quia haec justi non ex lege,sed spiritu fidei semper habuerunt. Quidquid perDominum venit, plenitudo est, cujus pars fuit pereumdem. Sicut parvulus, qui cum nihil minus habeata viro, tamen vir non est, et per incrementa nonnovorum, sed eorumdem membrorum, in eum venitplenitudo corporis, ut sit perfectus, idem tamen quifuerat parvulus. Revera non erat in omnibus Spiritussanctus ante passionem Domini; sed in illis quiper ipsum praesentem credebant, ut ipso victore, etcuncta perficiente, signati perficerentur. Nam justi,quos hic invenit, habuerunt Spiritum sanctum, utSimeon et Nathanael, et Zacharias, et Elisabeth, etAnna vidua filia Phanuel. Promissio a lege separataest; neque cum sit diversa, immisceri potest.

Nonconditio infirmat promissionem; cogimur autem nosloqui ea, quae sine igne doloris audire non possumus.Dicunt enim quidam, qui promissionum firmitatem,et quae ex lege est, transgressionem nesciunt:promisisse quidem Deum Abrahae, omnes gentes (sedsalvo libero arbitrio), si legem custodissent. Et sipericula imperitiae quorumdam justorum salute patefaceréprodest; sed cum de Deo omnipotente sermoest, moderari dicenda debemus, ne silenda reputandomemoremus, et ex ore nostro, aliena licet, audiantur.Quare cum tremore loquentes, sua cuique periculaconsideranda relinquamus. Manifestum est,praescisse Deum, futuros de libero arbitrio, quosAbrahae promisit, aut non futuros. Alterum est duorum:si futuros, finita quaestio est; si non futuros,[29] fidelis Deus non promitteret. Aut si hoc est statutumapud Deum, tunc promissos dare, si promissivellent: profecto diceret, ne servus ejus ac credens,quia, quod promisit, potens est et facere, ludificareturAbraham. Promissio autem illa est, quae nihilconditionis incurrit. Sin minus; nec promissio estfirma, nec fides integra. Quid enim stabile remanebitin Dei promissione, aut in Abrahae fide, si id, quodpromissum et creditum est, in eorum, qui promissisunt, penderet arbitrio? Ergo et Deus alienum promisit,et Abraham incaute credidit. Ut quid etiamipsa promissio, debitum postmodum facta est, dicenteDeo: Benedicentur in te omnes gentes terrae, proeo quod audisti vocem meam, et non pepercisti filio tuodilecto propter me (Gen. XXII, 18)? Neque autem exhis, quibus facile est, et adversum Abrahae meritumliberi arbitrii calumnia strepere; etiam post mortemipsius Abrahae, debitorem se ipsius confirmatDeus, et propter eum, se facturum, quodejus filio promittebat, dicens: Ero tecum, etbenedicam te. Tibi enim et semini tuo dabo terramhanc, et statuam jurationem meam, quam juraviAbrahae patri tuo, et multiplicabo semen tuum sicutstellas coeli, et dabo tibi et semini tuo omnes gentesterrae, pro eo quod audivit Abraham pater tuus vocemmeam (Gen. XXVI, 3-5). Ecce firmatum est debitumAbrahae. Non enim potuit per liberum arbitrium,post mortem amittere, quod vivus meruerat; nolueruntautem gentes credere. Quid faciet Abraham,cui debetur? quomodo accipiet fidei et tentationissuae debitum, cujus debere Deo securus fuit? Cuisi dictum est: Dabo quod promisi, et reddam quodjuravi (Ibid., 4): si voluerint gentes, non crederet,sed exspectaret fortuitum. Si conditione opus est,cum operario esse debet, non cum mercede. Operariusenim potest velle accipere aut nolle, non mercesreddi aut non reddi. Omnes enim gentes inmercedem fidei datae sunt Abrahae, sicut Deus dicit:Merces tua multa est (Gen. XV, 1). Non enim si futuriessent, et non quia futuri erant, promisit.Quia non propter fidem Abrahae, placuit Deo, salvasfore omnes gentes: quas non modo ante fidemAbrahae, sed ante mundi constitutionem possedit. Sedquaesivit fidelem, cui id donaret, ex quo esset, cuiid futurum statuerat. Abraham ergo non id meruit,ut essent, qui futuri erant, quos Deus elegerat, etconformes imaginis filii sui futuros esse praeviderat.In Genesi namque de praescientia Dei omnes gentesAbrahae promissas, Scriptura testatur, dicens:Abraham autem fiens fiet, et erit in gentem magnam etmultam et benedicentur in eo omnes gentes terrae (Gen.XXVI, 16). Sciebat etiam quia disponebat Abrahamfiliis suis, et domui suae post se, ut custodiant viasDomini, facere justitiam et judicium, ut superducatDeus in Abraham quaecumque locutus est ad eum.Invenimus autem et conditiones, ut: Si me audieritis,et volueritis. Ubi praescientia Dei, ubi firmitaspromissionis in hujusmodi conditionibus? Dixitetiam Apostolus, propterea ex fide, et non ex lege,datam esse promissionem, ut firma esset promissio(Rom. IV, 16). Lex, inquit, iram operatur; ubi etiamnon est lex, neque transgressio (Ibid., 15). Proptereaex fide ut secundum gratiam firma esset promissioomni semini. Recte, ut firma esset promissio. Adjecitenim, conditione non est firma. Satis enim stultumest credere, in totum corpus convenire, quod bipartitocorpori dicitur. Absit ut his dicat Deus: Sime audieritis, quos sciebat audituros, quos antequamfaceret, noverat in imagine Dei perseveraturos,quos et promisit. Non est data conditio, id est lex,nisi impiis et peccatoribus: ut aut ad gratiam confugiant,aut justius puniantur, si irritam fecerint.Ut quid lex ad justos, quibus lex non est posita, quipropitio Deo legem sine lege faciunt, qui serviunt,quid ad imaginem et similitudinem Dei et Christivivunt, qui volentes, boni sunt? Qui enim sub legeest, metu mortis, non est talis, misericors, non estimago Dei. Displicet illi lex: sed timet ultricem, necperficere potest; quod non voto, sed necessitate faciendumputat. Tradatur necesse est, propriae voluntati;ut voluntas profecto praemium recipiat,quia animam non miscuit voluntati Dei. Displicetilli, quod Deus voluit. Etenim voluntate malus est,qui necessitate bonus est. Lex operi impedimentumest, non voluntati. Non est conjunctus Deo, qui simali poena non esset, malum sequeretur. Nec voluntatemDei facit, qui gemit quod non suam faciat.Non est misericors, qui timet esse crudelis. Sublege est, servus est. Non furtum odit, sed poenammetuit. Furetur autem necesse est, persuasus etvictus, qui carnalis est sub virtute peccati, SpiritumDei non habens. Qui autem amat bonum, imagoDei est, fide Dominica vivit, et haeres, jam non estancillae filius (Gal. IV, 30, 31), qui accepit legem intimore; sed liberae, secundum Isaac, qui non accepitSpiritum servitutis in timore: sed adoptionem filiorum,clamantem Abba pater (Rom. VIII, 15).

Qui diligitDeum, non timet serviliter. Scriptum est, timorenim servilis, cum odio est disciplinae. Filiiautem cum honore patris. Aliud est timere ex lege,aliud pro veneratione tremendae Dei majestatis.Ejusmodi similes sunt patri suo, qui in coelis: commemoratiet docti amant bonum, oderunt malum.Sine lege sunt, liberi sunt, ipsi promissi sunt: nonipsi dicitur: Si me audieritis, potest etenim audire:numquid conveniet in eum, quem Deus nondumpraevidit auditurum? Et justi quidem, quos Deuspraesciit (Ibid., 29), sunt in ista lege. Dicitur et ipsis:si me audieritis; sed alia causa, non quia possunt nonaudire: sed ut semper solliciti sint suae salutis, etcerti exitus sui. Non enim securus est unusquisqueex numero se esse praescitorum, Apostolo dicente:Ne ipse reprobus fiam (I Cor. IX, 27). Non est ergoillis, irae operatrix ista lex, sed fidei exercitium,quo jugiter Dei gratiam quaerant laborantes, ut perficiaturquod in illis Deus praevidit, et de libero arbitriofuerint in vitam destinati. Alias impossibile estnon audire eum, quem Deus auditurum praevidit,promisit, juravit. In quam vero partem lex proprieconveniat, licet uni detur corpori, Dominus inEvangelio declarat, dicens Apostolis: Si haec scitis,beati estis si feceritis ea. Non de omnibus dico vobis:Ego scio, quos elegi (Joan. XIII, 17, 18). Magna brevitasostendentis unum corpus et separantis. Si enimdiceret: Non de omnibus vobis dico; aut, non deomnibus dico, non ostenderet unum corpus. Nuncautem non de omnibus dico: ostendit quia et si nonde omnibus, de illis tamen dixit. Sicut quis dicat,non de toto te dixi, duo enim corpora mixta sunt,velut unum, et in commune, unum corpus laudaturaut increpatur. Sicut in Exodo, cum quidam contravetitum, Sabbatis existet ut manna colligeret, aitDeus Moysi: Quousque non vultis audire legem meam(Exod. XVI, 26)? cum Moyses semper audierit. Quidde illa lege dicimus, quae aperte promissioni videturadversa? Scriptum est in Isaia: Si me audisses, Israel,esset sicut arena maris numerus tuus (Isa. XLVIII, 18).Ecce increpatur Israel, quod vitio suo non fueritfactus sicut arena maris. Superest intelligere, quia sisemper non audierit, semper exiguus erit. Et ubifirmitas promissionum? Sed hoc fit, quia prius volumusintelligere, quam credere et fidem rationisubjicere. Si autem credamus omnimodo ita fieri,ut Deus juravit, dabit rationem fides. Quam perfidumest ratione quaerere, et intelligimus firmitatemmajorem esse promissionum, quam putamus infirmitatem.Hoc enim dictum: Si audisset Israel, commemoratioest justitiae Dei, et confirmatio promissionum,dispositione Dei quosdam factos ad mortem,quosdam vero ad vitam. Propterea, praesentibusdixit, Si me audissetis: ut manifestum fieret, quiaquos promisit, ut arenam futuros, ideo promisit,quia praevidit audituros. Ante Dominum enim Christum,cum hoc dictum est, [30] numquam fuit semen Abrahae, sicut arena maris? Quod probare facile est. Primum, quia in Christo promisit hanc multitudinem: Non in seminibus quasi in multis, sed quasi in uno, et semini tuo, quod est Christus (Gal. III, 16). Deinde, quia omnes gentes promisit, quod ante Christum fieri non potuit. Et si fuit ante Dominum numerus filiorum Israel sicut arena maris: sed cum falsis fratribus, qui non sunt filii Abrahae. Non enim, quia omnes ex Abraham, omnes filii Abrahae; aut quia Israel, omnes Israel. Sicut Apostolus, cum se Anathema optaret esse pro Israel (Rom. IX, 3), quorum esset filiorum adoptio et testamenta, ostendit, non esse cujusmodi filios Abrahae, sed de affectu carnalis necessitudinis dolere, quod ex ipso numero non essent. Non quod promissio Dei excidisset, dicens: Non tamen excidit sermo Dei, non enim omnes, qui sunt ex Israel, hi sunt Israel, neque quia sunt semen Abrahae, omnes filii sunt: sed in Isaac vocabitur tibi semen: id est, non qui sunt filii carnis, hi sunt filii Dei: sed filii promissionis deputantur in semen (Ibid., 6-8). Ergo in antiqua multitudine non fuit Abrahae semen: nisi illis, qui secundum Isaac fidei et promissionis filii erant. Etiam hoc exemplum inducit: Si fuerit numerus filiorum Israel, sicut arena maris: reliquiae liberabuntur, id est, exiguum (Isa. X, 12: Ose. I, 10). Et, nisi Dominus sabaoth reliquisset nobis semen, sicut Sodoma essemus (Isa. I, 9). Ipsae reliquiae fuerunt semen Abrahae: ne omnis Judaea, ut Sodoma esset. Iterum cum assereret, numquam Deum haereditatem suam reliquisse: sed sicut in adventu Domini, pars Israel salva facta est: ita semper fuisse. Quid, inquit, dicit responsum divinum? Reliqui mihi septem millia vivorum, qui non curvaverunt genu ante Bahal (III Reg. XVIII, 19; Rom. XI, 4). Sic nunc reliquiae secundum electionem salvae factae sunt, dicendo: Si nunc in hoc tempore: ostendit et ante sic factum in Israel, ut reliquiae, idest, modicum salvum fieret. Si autem, nec fides, nec ratio persuadet fidei, qui promissus fuerat, dictum esse: Si me audisses, Israel; esset sicut arena maris numerus tuus (Isa. XLVIII, 18). Et Jacob, qui antequam nasceretur, datus est: idem libero arbitrio postmodum reprobatus est. Sicut Osee dicit: Judicium Domini ad Judam, ut vindicet in Jacob, secundum vias ejus, et secundum studia ejus retribuet ei (Ose. XII, 2): quia in utero supplantavit fratrem suum, et in laboribus suis invaluit ad Deum, et invaluit cum angelo, potens factus est (Gen. XXV, 23; Rom. IX, 10). Si autem constat, in Jacob dilectum consummasse, non est idem qui in laboribus invaluit ad Deum et supplantator, sed duo in uno corpore. Figura est enim duplicis seminis Abrahae, id est duorum populorum in uno utero matris Ecclesiae luctantium. Unus est, secundum electionem de praescientia dilectus: Alter electione suae voluntatis, iniquus.

Jacob autem et Esau, in uno suntcorpore, ex uno semine. Sed quod perspicue duoprocreati sunt: ostensio est duorum populorum. Etne quis putaret, ita perspicue fore separatos duospopulos: ostensum est, ambos in uno corpore futurosin Jacob, qui et dilectus vocatus est, et fratrissupplantator expressus. Itaque in duobus quantitasexpressa est, non qualitas separationis.Caeterum, ambo qui separati sunt in uno futuri,antequam dividuntur, ostensi sunt. Et Isaac, venit,inquit, frater tuus cum dolo, et accepit benedictionemtuam (Gen. XXVII, 35). Nisi ita locutio mystica sit,breviter ostendentis duo in uno corpore: nonnecontra rationem est, ut benedictionem in proximumdolose acceperit, Scriptura dicente: Qui non juravitproximo in dolo; iste accipiet benedictionem a Domino(Psal. XXIII, 4)? Numquam autem Jacob, idest Ecclesia venit ad benedictionem, non comitantedolo, id est, falsis fratribus. Sed non, quia innocentiaet dolus simul veniunt ad benedictionem, simulbenedicuntur: quia qui potest capere, capiat(Matth. XIX, 12), et unum semen pro qualitate terrae,provenit. Non est autem contrarium, quod malumfratrum videtur supplantasse, quia non dixit: Inutero supplantavit Esau, sed fratrem suum. Esau autem,ubique signum est, et nomen malorum: Jacobautem, utrorumque: illa ratione, quod parsmala simulet se Jacob, et sine dubio, uno nomine:pars autem bona, non potest se simulare Esau. Esthoc nomen malorum tantum: illud vero bipartitum.Caeterum de libero arbitrio, nec Jacob omne semenbonum, nec Esau omne malum, sed ex utroqueutrumque. Ex Abraham ita bipartitum semen ostensumest. Natum est unum ex ancilla in figura (Gal.IV, 22): ut ostenderetur etiam servos futuros exAbraham, et recessit cum sua matre. Postquam verorecessit, inventum est in alterius semine, quod estex libera, quod est ex Israel, qui accepit legem inmonte Sina, quod est Agar in servitute generans. Illicin eodem populo secundum Isaac ex libera promissionisfilii, id est, sancti et fideles multi procreatisunt. Separatis itaque a credentibus figuris Israel etEsau, in uno populo totum postmodum provenit.Illic ab origine utrumque testamentum Agar et Isaac;sed pro tempore alterum sub alterius nomine delituitet delitescit, quia neque revelato novo quiescit vetusgenerando. Non ergo dixit, Agar, quae in servitutemgenerans. Oportet autem simul ambos crescere usquead messem. Sicut ergo tunc sub professione veterisTestamenti latuit novum, id est, gratia, quodsecundum Isaac promissionis filios generaret ex libera,quod in Christo revelatum est: ita et nuncobtinente nova, non desunt servitutis filii generanteAgar, quod in Christo revelabitur. Confirmat Apostolus,id nunc quoque inter fratres geri, quod tuncinter illos gerebatur, dicens: Vos autem, fratres secundumIsaac, promissionis filii estis. Sed sicut tunc,qui secundum carnem natus est, persequebatur spiritualem,ita et nunc (Ibid. 28, 29). Et necessarioaddidit, sed quid dicit Scriptura? Expelle ancillamet filium ejus: non enim cohaeres erit filius ancillae,filio liberae (Ibid., 30). Quod autem dixit, sicut tuncpersequebatur; ita et nunc, non est inane. Apostolusenim interpretatus est persequebatur. Nam Scripturadicit: Ludebat Ismael cum Isaac (Gen. XXI, 9).Numquid fratres, qui circumcisiones Galatis praedicebat,aperte illos, et non per lusum, id est, sineindicio persecutionis insequebatur? Sicut ergo degenere ludendi persecutorem dixit: ita et istos, quiFilios Dei, velut per communem utilitatem, id est,disciplinam legis, a Christo separare, et matri suaeAgar, filios militant. Alia enim non est causa, quafilii diaboli irrepant, ad explorandam libertatemnostram, et simulent se fratres, et in Paradiso nostrovelut Dei filios ludere: quam de subacta libertatefiliorum Dei glorientur, qui portabunt judicium,qualescumque illi fuerint, qui omnem sanctum persecutisunt, qui prophetas occiderunt, qui semperSpiritui sancto restiterunt; inimici crucis Christi,negantes Christum in carne, dum ejus membraoderunt, corpus peccati, filii exterminii, ministeriumfacinoris, qui veniunt secundum operationemSatanae in omni virtute, signis et prodigiis, spiritualianequitiae in coelestibus: quos Dominus Christus,quem in carne persequuntur, interficiet spirituoris sui, et destruet manifestatione adventus sui.Tempus est enim, quod haec non [31] ministeriis, sedaperte dicantur, imminente discessione, quod estrevelatio hominis peccati, discedente Lot a Sodomis.

Regula IV

De specie et genere.

Lux allata Ezechiel, capp. XXVII et XXXII et XXXVIet XXXVII, Isai. XIII et XXIV, Hierem. XXV. De specie et genere loquimur, non secundum virtutemRhetoricam humanae sapientiae, quam quimagis omnibus potuit, locutus non est, ne crucemChristi fecisset inanem, si auxilio atque ornamentosermonis, ut falsitas, indiguisset. Sed loquimur secundummysteria coelestis sapientiae magisterio Spiritussancti. Qui in quod veritatis pretium fidemconstituerit mysterii, narravit in speciem genus abscondens,ut in veterem Hierusalem, totam, quaenunc est per orbem Ecclesiam assumeret, aut inunum membrum, totum corpus, ut in Salomone.Sed hoc non minus occultum est, quam caetera, quaenon solum specie verbi, sed etiam multiformi narrationeoccultantur. Quamobrem, Dei gratia inauxilium postulata; elaborandum nobis est, ut spiritusmultiplicet ingressus legendi, eloquiumquesubtile, quod ad impedimentum intellectus, specieigenus, aut generi speciem inserit: genus species nesit, facile possit videri. Dum enim speciem narrat,ita in genus transit, ut transitus non statim liquidoappareat: sed talia transiens ponit verba, quae inutrumque conveniant, donec paulatim speciei modumexcedat, et transitus dilucidet, cum, quae a speciecoeperant, nonnisi in genus convenerint, et eodemmodo genus relinquit, in speciem rediens. Aliquandoautem a specie in genus non supradicto modo revertitur.Aliquando supradicto modo transit, et evidenterrevertitur simili ordinis varietate: aut aspecie in genus, aut a genere in speciem, finit narrationem.Aliquando redit ex hoc in illud non semel:et omnis narratio nec speciem excedit, nec genuspraeterit, in utrumque conveniens. Haec varietastranslationis et ordinis exigit fidem, quae gratiam Deiquaerat. Sic Dominus per Ezechielem loquitur, et regibuseorum, qui ab Hierusalem capti et dispersifuerant, gentium jungit adventum, et in terra, quamPatres nostri possederunt, exprimit mundum. Septemenim gentes Abrahae promissae, figura sunt omniumgentium. Factus est, inquit, ad me sermo Domini,dicens: Fili hominis, domus Israel habitaverunt interra, et polluerunt illam in via sua, et in idolis suiset peccatis: secundum immunditiam menstruatae factaest via eorum ante faciem meam. Et effudi iram meamsuper eos, et dispersi illos inter nationes, quas ingressisunt, et polluerunt illic nomen meum sanctum: dumdicunt ipsi, populus Domini hi, et de terra tua egressisunt: et peperci illis, propter nomen tuum sanctum,quod polluerunt domus Israel in nationibus, in quasingressi sunt illic. Propter hoc, dic domui Israel: Haecdicit Dominus: Non vobis ego facio, domus Israel:sed propter nomen sanctum quod polluistis in nationibus,in medio quarum ingressi estis. Illic incipitjungere genus: Et sanctificabo nomen meum, sanctumillud magnum, quod pollutum est inter nationes, quodpolluistis in medio earum, et scient gentes, quoniamego sum Dominus, qui sanctificabor in vobis ante oculoseorum, et accipiam vos de gentibus, et congregabo vosex omnibus terris, et inducam vos in terram vestram.Aperte excedit speciem: Et aspergam vos aqua munda,et mundabimini ab omnibus simulacris vestris, et mundabovos, et dabo vobis cor novum, et spiritum novumdabo in vos, et auferam cor lapideum de carne vestra:et dabo vobis carneum, et spiritum meum dabo in vos,et faciam, ut in justitiis meis ambuletis, et judiciamea custodiatis, et operemini. Et habitabitis interra quam dedi patribus vestris. Et eritis mihi in populum,et ego ero vobis in Deum, et mundabo vos exomnibus immunditiis vestris (Ezech. XXXVI, 17, 28).Attingit speciem, non tamen relinquens genus: Etvocabo triticum, et multiplicabo illud: et non dabo invos famem, et multiplicabo fructum ligni, et quae nascunturin agro: ut non accipiatis ultra opprobriumfamis, in nationibus, et reminiscemini vias vestraspessimas, cogitationes vestras non bonas, et non odietiseas ante faciem eorum in iniquitatibus vestris, et inabominationibus eorum. Non propter vos, ego facio,dicit Dominus. Notum est vobis, confundimini et revertiminide viis vestris, domus Israel. Haec dicitAdonai Dominus: In die, qua mundabo vos ab omnibusiniquitatibus vestris, et inebriari faciam civitates,in figura terrae Judae, quae bellis vastata fuerat, coletur,propter quod fuit exterminata sub oculis omnispraetereuntis. Et dicent, Terra illa, quae fuerat exterminata,facta est sicut hortus deliciarum, et civitates desertaeet exterminatae et demolitae, munitae consederunt.Et scient gentes, quaecumque derelictae fuerint in circuituvestro, quoniam ego sum Dominus. Aedificavidemolitas, et plantavi exterminatas: quia ego Dominuslocutus sum et feci (Ibid. 29, 38).Apostolus quoque ingressu Jacob promissum esseintroitum gentium, sic interpretatur dicens, Donecplenitudo gentium intret, et sic omnis Israel salvabitur,sicut scriptum est: Veniet a Sion, qui liberet etauferat impietates ab Jacob (Rom. XI, 25, 26). Eteodem genere locutionis redit in speciem, dicens:Secundum Evangelium quidem inimici propter vos.Item in Ezechiele incipit ab specie, quae conveniatet in genus, et finit in solo genere, ostendens, terrampatrum mundi esse possessionem: Haec dicitDominus: Ecce ego accipiam omnem domum Israelde medio gentium, in quas ingressi sunt illic, et congregaboeos ab omnibus qui sunt in circuitu eorum, etinducam eos in terram Israel, et princeps unus eriteorum. Et non erunt ultra in duas gentes, nec dividenturultra in duo regna: ne contaminentur adhuc insimulacris suis. Et liberabo eos ab omnibus iniquitatibuseorum, quibus peccaverunt in eis, et emundaboeos, et erunt mihi in populum, et ego Dominus ero illisin Deum (Ezech. XXXVII, 21, 23).Aperte transit in genus: Et servus meus Davidprinceps in medio eorum erit, Pastor unus omnium,qui in praeceptis meis ambulabunt, et judicia mea custodient,et facient ea, et inhabitabunt in terra sua, quamego dedi servo meo Jacob, ubi habitaverunt patres eorum,et habitabunt in ea ipsi, et David servus meusprinceps eorum in saecula, et disponam illis testamentumpacis, et testamentum aeternum erit cum illis.Et ponam sancta mea in medio eorum in saecula, eterit habitatio mea in illis, et ero illis Deus: et ipsi eruntmihi populus. Et scient gentes, quia ego sum Dominusqui sanctifico eos, dum sunt sancta in medio eorum, dicitDominus

(Ibid., 24, 28). Item illic egressui dispersionisIsrael, gentium inserit adventum.Eremum figuram fuisse populi deserti, in quoEcclesia nunc esse, manifestatur: et quod iidemmali quamvis una cum populo Dei ex gentibus revocenturin terram Israel, tamen in terra non sint.Vivo ego, dicit Dominus, si respondero vobis, et si ascenderitin cor vestrum hoc, et non erit, quemadmodumdicitis vos. Erimus sicut gentes, et sicut tribus terrae,ut serviamus lignis et lapidibus. Vivo ego, dicit Dominus,nisi in manu forti et brachio excelso, et in iraeffusa regnabo super vos, et educam vos de populis etrecipiam vos de regionibus, in quibus dispersi estis inmanu forti et brachio excelso, et ira effusa, et adducamvos in desertum populorum, et disputabo ad vos faciead faciem: quemadmodum disputavi ad patres vestrosin deserto terrae Aegypti, sic judicabo vos, dicit Dominus,et redigam vos sub virga mea, et inducam vos in[32] numero, et eligam impios de vobis et desertores:quoniam ex transmigratione eorum educam eos, et interram Israel non intrabunt, et cognoscetis, quia egosum Dominus (Ezech. XX, 31, 38).Item illi captivitati montium Israel promittit Deusubertatem, et multiplicationem populorum usque infinem: Quoniam, inquit, dederunt terram tuam sibiin possessionem cum jucunditate inhonorantes animas,atque exterminaverunt in vastationem: propterea, prophetasuper terram Israel, et dic montibus et collibus,et rivis et nemoribus: Haec dicit Dominus: Ecce egoin zelo meo, et in ira mea locutus sum, propter quodopprobrium gentium portatis. Ecce ego levabo manummeam super nationes, quae sunt in circuitu vestro. Hiinjuriam suam accipient: vestri autem montes, Israel,uvam et fructum vestrum manducabit populus meus,qui appropinquat venire. Quia ecce ego super vos, etcolemini, et seminabimini: et multiplicabo super vostotam domum Israel usque in finem, et habitabunturcivitates, et quae desolatae erant, aedificabuntur (Ezech.XXXVI, 5, 10). Item illic velut in novissima resurrectione,prima significatur: Locutus est, inquit, ad me,dicens: Fili hominis, ossa haec, omnis domus Israel est.Ipsi dicunt: Arida facta sunt ossa nostra, interiit spesnostra, exspiravimus. Propterea propheta et dic; Haecdicit Dominus: Ecce ego aperiam monumenta vestra,et educam vos de monumentis vestris, et inducam vosin terram Israel, et scietis, quia ego Dominus, cumaperiam sepulcra vestra, et educam de monumentis populummeum, et dabo spiritum meum in vos, et vivetis:et ponam vos super terram vestram, et scietisquia ego sum Dominus (Ezech. XXXVII, 11, 14).Numquid perspicue, cum resurrexerimus, tuncsciemus Dominum, et non nunc, cum per baptismumresurgimus? Aut mortui poterunt dicere: Aridafacta sunt ossa nostra (Ibid., 11), ut merito mortuisid promissum esse credamus?

Quid enim est sacramenti,ne in ambiguum veniret, aperuit Deus. Namde novissima carnis resurrectione, neminem Christianumcredimus dubitare. Et Dominus secundumJoannem has resurrectiones manifestat, dicens:Amen dico vobis: quia, qui verbum meum audit, etcredit ei, qui misit me, habet vitam aeternam, et in judiciumnon veniet, sed transiet a morte ad vitam.Amen dico vobis, quoniam venit hora et nunc est,quando mortui audient vocem filii Dei, et qui audierint,vivent. Sicut enim habet Pater vitam in se: sicdedit Filio vitam habere in semetipso. Et potestatemdedit ei et judicium facere: quia filius hominis est(Joan. V, 24, 27). Jungit novissimam resurrectionem:Nolite mirari hoc: quia venit hora, in qua omnes,qui in monumentis sunt, audient vocem Filii Dei,et exient qui bona fecerunt, in resurrectionem vitae:qui autem mala fecerunt, in resurrectionem judicii(Ibid., 28, 29). Primo dixit, mortui qui audierint, vivent.Secundo, omnes, qui in monumentis sunt, exient.Item quod in uno homine totum corpus significetur,in Regum libro promittit Deus David, de Salomonedicens: Suscitabo regnum ejus: ipse aedificabit mihidomum (II Reg. VII, 15).Conveniunt ista: sed excedit speciem, dicens:Et dirigam thronum ejus usque in aeternum. Item inutrumque: Ego ero ei in patrem, et ipse erit mihi infilium. Et si venerit injustitia ejus, arguam eum invirga hominum, et in artibus filiorum hominum; misericordiamautem meam non auferam ab eo, sicut abstuli,a quibus abstuli a conspectu meo, et fidelis fietdomus ejus. Iterum excedit speciem: et regnum ejusin aeternum in conspectu meo, et fidelis fiet domusejus. Iterum excedit speciem: et regnum ejus inaeternum in conspectu meo, et thronus ejus erit confirmatususque in aeternum (Ibid., 13, 16). Quodautem videtur in excessus specie thronum Christipromittere in aeternum, thronum filii hominis promittit,et ita Corpus Christi, id est, Ecclesiae. Nonenim propter David promisit Deus regnaturum Christum:cui ante constitutionem mundi promisit hancclaritatem. Et per Isaiam sic dicit Deus Christo:Magnum tibi erit istud: ut voceris puer meus, et statuastribus Jacob, et Israel dispersionem convertas.Ecce posui te in testamentum generis, in lumen gentium,ut sis in salutem usque in novissimum terrae(Isa. XLIX, 6). Quid majus Filio Dei vocari puer meus,et Israel dispersionem convertere, aut per cumfactum esse ipsum Israel et coelum et terram, etquae in eis sunt visibilia et invisibilia? Sed ei dixitmagnum esse, qui Filio Dei mixtus est ex semineDavid. Omnis enim promissio Abrahae et David,ipsa est, ut semen eorum misereretur ei, cujus suntomnia, et esset cohaeres in aeternum: non proptereos regnaret Christus, qui est omnium rex a Patreconstitutus. Quid dicimus de Salomone? cum Deoest, an post idololatriam reprobatus est? Si cumDeo dixerimus: impunitatem spondebimus idolorumcultoribus. Non enim dicit Scriptura, poenitentiamegisse Salomonem, aut recepisse sapientiam. Si autemreprobatum dixerimus: occurrit vox Dei, quaedicit, nec terrae quidem regnum auferre Salomonipropter David, sicut scriptum est in libro Regum:Disrumpens disrumpam regnum tuum de manu tua:et dabo illud servo tuo. Verum, in diebus tuis non faciamhaec, propter David patrem tuum. De manu filiitui accipiam illud. Verum omne regnum non accipiam,sceptrum unum dabo filio tuo: propter David servummeum, et propter Hierusalem civitatem, quam elegi,(III Reg. XI, 11, 14). Quid enim prodest David, sipropter eum filius ejus regnum terrae consequeretur,coeleste perditurus? Quo manifestum est, cumDeo esse Salomonem: cui regnum quidem terraeablatum non est propter David, quod et dixerat:Arguam in virga hominum peccata ejus: misericordiamautem meam non auferam ab eo (II Reg. VII, 14).Quod si neque reprobatus est, neque idolorum cultoresregnum Dei possident: manifestuum est, figuramfuisse Ecclesiae bipartitae, Salomonem, cujuslatitudo cordis et sapientia, sicut arena maris, etidololatria horribilis. Disrumpens, inquit, disrumpamregnum tuum de manu tua: verum in diebus tuis non faciam.De manu filii tui accipiam illud. Jugis operationisest, disrumpens disrumpam: sicut benedicens benedicam,et multiplicans multiplicabo semen tuum. Ostenditenim semper futurum Salomonem in filio, id est,in posteris: cujus posthumis Salomonis temporibusnon aufert Deus regnum, secundum promissa Patrum:sed corrigit illud usque in aeternum, ut auferatjugiter secundum idolatriam Salomonis, insuo peccato perseverantis. Alias, quomodo de manuSalomonis disrumpens disrumpit aut non disrumpit,si non nunc est Salomon in filiis bonus aut malus?Quod autem dicit: Verum, non omne regnum accipio:in speciem redit, incipiens aliam figuram infilio Salomonis et servo. In Jesu Nave quoque sicdicit Dominus, manifestans in uno homine futurumcorpus ostendit: sed hoc loco malum tantummodo.Peccavit, inquit, populus et transgressus testamentum,quod disposui ad illos, furati sunt de anathemate, miseruntin vasa sua (Jos. VIII, 11): cum solus Acharde tribu Juda id fecisset. Quod corpus semper futurumintelligens Jesus, sic ait, cum eum occideret:Exterminet te Deus sicut et hodie (Ibid., 25). Illudautem multo magis necessarium est scire: omnesomnino civitates Israel et gentium, vel provinciasquas Scriptura alloquitur, aut in quibus aliquid gestumrefert figuram esse Ecclesiae. Aliquas quidempartis malae tantum, aliquas bonae, aliquas veroutriusque. Et si sint aliqua, quae etiam in gentes,quae foris sunt videantur convenire: in parte tamen,quae intus est, convenitur omne corpus adversum,sicut in Israel captivo, promittitur gentibusad Deum reditus. Impossibile est enim legem loquiei, qui in lege non est: de eo loqui, ad ipsumtamen non: et sive alicubi sine ista occasione nonin Israel specialiter alienigenas alloquitur, intusomnimodo credendi sunt: quoniam, etsi eveniebatspecialiter quod prophetatum est, Ecclesia tamen est.Proprietas denique non omnibus speciebus [33] convenit.Nam et Damascus et Tyrus et Soor et aliae multaeusque nunc exstant, quas Deus penitus tolli, necrestaurari dixerat. In alienigenis autem civitatibusEcclesiam conveniri apertum est in Ezechiele, cuicum Dominus diceret, praedicere interitum in Theman,quae est Esau, et in Dagon, quod est idolumallophylorum, intellexit parabolam esse adversumHierusalem et templum. Factus est, inquit, sermoDomini ad me, dicens: Fili hominis, confirma faciemtuam super Theman, respice in Dagon, propheta insilvam summam Nages: Audi verbum Domini. Haecdicit Dominus: Ecce, ego incendam in te ignem, etcomedet in te omne lignum viride, et omne lignumaridum. Non exstinguetur flamma incensa et cumbureturin ea omnis facies a subsolano usque ad aquilonem, utcognoscat omnis caro, quia ego Dominus succendi illud,non exstinguetur ultra. Et dixi, non, Domine. Ipsi dicuntad me: Nonne parabola est haec, quae dicitur(Ezech. XX, 45, 49)? Et factus est, inquit, sermo Dominiad me, dicens: Propterea, fili hominis, prophetaet confirma faciem tuam ad Hierusalem, respicienssancta eorum: et prophetabis super terram Israel. Haecdicit Dominus: Ecce ego educam gladium meum devagina sua: et disperdam de te inimicum et injustum.Sic exiet gladius meus de vagina sua super omnem carnema subsolano usque ad aquilonem, et sciet omniscaro, quia ego sum Dominus, qui emisi gladium meumde vagina sua, non egredietur ultra. Confirma, inquit,faciem tuam, super Theman, et respice in Dagon(Ezech. XXI, 1, 5). Et interpretatus est dicens: Confirmafaciem tuam ad Hierusalem, et respice in sanctaeorum. Et ostendit in omnem Hierusalem, dicens:Disperdam de te inimicum et injustum. Ita futurumgeneraliter ait: Sic exiet gladius meus super omnemcarnem a subsolano usque ad aquilonem. Ostendit inHierusalem esse Theman, quam illic Deus interficit,et Dagon, et omnia exsecrabilia gentium operantefilio David Salomone in filiis suis, quo etiam evidenterdejecta templa Dei et demolita, atque spiritualiterexusta, projecit in torrentem, id est, saeculum,qui nascitur filius David Josias, ut disrumpaturaltare in Bethel, sicut scriptum est: Altare, altare,haec dicit Dominus, Ecce filius nascetur de domo David:Josias nomen illi (III Reg. XIII, 2). Ninive civitasalienigenarum, bipartitae Ecclesiae figura est.Sed quia ordinem lectionem interpretando prosequi,longum est: satis erit, quod specie convenire nonpotest dicere. Erat, inquit, Ninive civitas magna(Jonae III, 3): adeo, cum esset adversa Deo, ut metropolisAssyriorum, quae et Samariam delevit,et omnem Judaeam semper oppressit: sed in figuraEcclesiae praedicante Jona, id est, Christo,omnis omnino liberata est. Eadem Ninive omninoinsequenti Propheta peritura describitur, cuipraedicans Dominus: Signum est Jonae in ventreceti (Matth. XII, 40; Luc. XI, 30). Atque ut et ipsePropheta ostendit, non esse illam civitatem specialem,interponit aliqua, quae speciei modum excedant.Non erat, inquit, finis gentilibus illius: cum esset civitasunius gentis. Et iterum: Multiplicasti mercatustuos super astra coeli, id est, Ecclesiam. Et iterum:Super quem non venit malitia tua semper? Numquidpotuit unius civitatis malitia, super omnem hominem,aut semper venisse, nisi illius, quam Cain fratrissanguine fundavit nomine filii sui, id est, posteritatis?Manifestius adhuc docet Propheta, Ecclesiamesse Ninive. Et extendet, inquit, manum suam in Aquilonem(id est, populum solis alienum adversus Meridianum)et perdet Assyrium (Soph. II, 13). Et illud:Ninive, exterminium sine aqua in desertum: et pascenturin medio ejus greges, omnes bestiae terrae et cameleonti,et hirci in laquearibus ejus cubabunt, et bestiaevocem dabunt in fossis ejus, et corvi in portis ejus,quoniam cedrus altitudo ejus. Civitas contemnens, quaehabitat in spe, quae dicit in corde suo: Ego sum, et nonest post me (Ibid., 13, 15). Et adhuc: Quomodo factaest in exterminio, pascua bestiarum? Omnis, qui transitper illam, sibilabit et movebit manus suas (Ib., 15).O illustris et redempta civitas, columba, quae audivitvocem, non recepit disciplinam, in Domino non estconfisa, et ad Dominum suum non appropinquavit.Principes ejus in ea, ut leones frementes; judicesejus, ut lupi Arabiae, non relinquentes inmane. Prophetae ejus, spiritu elati, viri contemptores.Sacerdotes ejus prophetant sacra, et [34] conscelerantlegem; Dominus autem justus, in templo ejus non facietinjustum (Soph. III, 1, 5). Aegyptus item bipartitaest. Ecce, inquit, Dominus sedet super nubemlevem, et venit in Aegyptum (Isa. XIX, 1, 3). [Nubes,corpus est spirituale post Baptismum, et claritas filiihominis. Primus est enim adventus Domini jugitercorpore suo venientis, sicut dicit: Amodo videbitisvenientem in nubibus coeli] et comminuentur manufactaAegypti a facie illius, et cor ipsorum minorabitur inillis, et exsurgent Aegyptii super Aegyptios et [35] expurgabithomo fratrem suum et homo proximum suum, etpugnabit civitas contra civitatem, et exsurget genssuper gentem (Matth. XXIV, 30), id est, Aegyptus superAegyptum, et lex supra legem, sensus scilicetdiversitate sub una lege: Et turbabitur spiritus Aegyptiorum in ipsis, et cogitationes eorum dispergam. Et postquam nunc generi speciem, nunc genus speciei miscuisset, adjecit, dicens: Die autem illo erit altare Domini in regione Aegyptiorum, et tituli ad terminos ejus Domino. Erit autem in signum in aeternum Domino, in regione Aegyptiorum (Isa. XIX, 19). Non dixit: licebit esse altare ad terminos Aegypti in aeternum: sed, erit. Ezechiel vero apertius ostendit totum mundum esse Aegyptum, dicens: O dies! quia prope est dies Domini, dies nubis, finis gentium erit: et veniet gladius super Aegyptios. Et jungit speciem: Et erit tumultus in Aethiopia, et cadent vulnerati in Aegypto, et cadent fundamenta ejus, Persae et Cretes, et Lydi, et omnes commesticii, et filii testamenti mei, gladio cadent in ea cum ipsis (Ezech. XXX. 3-5). Hoc autem factum est, cum post excidium descenderent in Aegyptum, et occiderent urillic a Nabuchodonosor secundum Hieremiae prophetationem. Fiet autem et generaliter, novissimo die, quando cum Aegyptiis filii testamenti ceciderint, Aegyptiorum more viventes. Item per Ezechielem minatur Deus regi Aegyptiorum, et ejus multitudini, quod essent terribiles in sanctos, inter circumcisos deputati: quod non convenit, nisi in eos, qui sibi circumcisione, id est, sacris blandiuntur. Quoniam igitur dedit timorem suum super terram vitae: ut dormiret in medio incircumcisorum vulneratus gladio Pharao, et omnis multitudo ejus cum ipso, dicit Dominus. Et illic a genere ad speciem: Haec dicit Dominus: Circumjaciam te super terram populorum multorum et extraham te in homomeo, et extendam te super campi tui: et constituam super te omnes aves coeli, et saturabo omnes bestias universae terrae: et dabo carnes tuas super montes, et saturabo sanguine tuo colles, et rigabitur terra ab his, quae de te procedunt; a multitudine tua in montibus vepres implebo abs te, et cooperiam coelum cum exstingueris, et obscurabo astra ejus, solem in nube contegam, et lunae non lucebit lumen ejus. Omnia quae lucent lumine in coelo obscurabuntur, et dabo tenebras super terram tuam, dicit Dominus. Jungit speciem: Et exasperabo cor populorum multorum: cum ducam captivitatem tuam in nationes, in terram, quam non noveras (Ezech. XXXII, 4-8). Excedit speciem: Et contristabuntur super te multae nationes, et reges earum, mentis alienatione stupebunt, cum volabit gladius meus super facies eorum, in medio eorum erit ad ruinam ex die ruinae tuae. Redit ad speciem: Quoniam haec dicit Dominus: Gladius regis Babylonis venit tibi in gladiis gigantum, et dejiciam virtutem tuam, pestes a nationibus omnes, et pendent contumeliam Aegypti, et conteretur omnis virtus ejus. In genus: Et perdam omnia pecora aqua multa: et non turbabit eam pes hominis ultra, et vestigium pecorum noncalcabit eam. Tunc requiescent aquae eorum, et fluminaeorum, ut oleum habebunt, dicit Dominus (Ibid.9-14). Species: Et dabo Aegyptum in interitum, etdesolabitur terra cum plenitudine sua, et dispergamomnes inhabitantes in ea (Ibid., 15). Genus: Et scient, quia ego Dominus sum. Operiam, inquit, coelum, cumexstingueris: et obscurabo astra ejus, solem in nubecontegam et lunae non lucebit lumen ejus. Omnia, quaelucent lumine in coelo obscurabuntur super te: et dabotenebras super terram tuam (Ezech. XXXII, 7, 8). [Inpassione Domini, non in terra Aegypti tantum fuerunttenebrae: sed in toto orbe. Sed nec, captaAegypto, obstupuerunt gentes, exspectantes ruinamsuam ex die ruinae ejus. Nam et de Soor sic scriptumest: Haec dicit Dominus ad Soor: Nonne, a dieruinae tuae, in gemitu vulneratorum, dum interficiunturgladio, in medio tui commovebuntur insulae, et discedenta sedibus suis omnes principes maris, et auferentmitras et vestem aurium suarum: dispoliabunt se in stupore mentis, stupebunt et timebunt in interitutuo, et ingemiscent super te, et accipient lamentationemet dicent tibi: Quomodo destructa est de mari civitasilla laudabilis, quae dedit timorem suum omnibus inhabitantibusin ea? et timebunt insulae ex die ruinae tuae(Ezech. XXVI, 15-18, sec. LXX): Ad clamorem vocistuae, gubernatores tui timore timebunt, et discedent denavibus omnes remiges tui et vectores et proretae marissuper terram stabunt, et ululabunt super te voce sua,et clamabunt super te amarum, et imponent super caputsuum terram, et cinerem sternent, et accipient superte lamentationem filiorum, lamentum Soor. Quantuminvenisti mercedis de mari? Satiasti gentes multitudinetua, et a commixtione tua locupletasti omnesreges terrae. Nunc autem contristata es in mari, in profundo aquae commixtio tua, et omnis congregatio tuain medio tui. Ceciderunt omnes remiges tui: omnesqui inhabitant insulas contristati sunt super te, et remigeseorum mentis alienatione stupuerunt, et lacrymatusest vultus eorum super te. Mercatores eorum de gentibusexsibilabunt te: perditio facta es, ultra non eris inaeternum, dicit Dominus (Ezech. XXVII, 28-36, sec.LXX).] Numquid in unam insulam conveniunt, quaedicta sunt: aut sola potuit locupletare omnes regesterrae? Sed aliqua relinquimus locis opportunis:quibus etsi strictim dicuntur, videri possunt. Tyrusbipartita est, sicut per Isaiam dicitur, qui post multaspeciei et generis, hoc quoque adjecit, dicens: Eritpost septuaginta annos Tyrus, sicut canticum fornicariae.Accipe citharam angularem, civitas fornicaria, oblita bene citharizare, multa cantica canta: ut tuicommemoratio fiat. Et erit post septuaginta annos,respectionem faciet Deus Tyri, et iterum restituetur inantiquum (Isa. XXIII, 15-17).] Numquid credibileest, universa regna terrarum, Tyrum venisse negetiandicausa? Quod si veniant; quae utilitas, praedixissefutura Tyro commercia omnibus regnis terrae,si non Tyrus, Ecclesia est, in qua omne terrarumnegotium est aeternae vitae? Sequitur enim et ostendit,quod sit ejus negotium, dicens: Et erit negotiatioejus et merces sancta Domino (Isa. XXIII, 15-17).Non enim in illis colligitur: sed illis, qui habitantin conspectu Domini. Omnis negotiatio ejus, edere etbibere et repleri, in signum memoriae in conspectu Domini(Ibid. 18). Si ergo negotiatio ejus, sancta Domino:quomodo potest omnibus esse regnis, nisiubique fuerit ista Tyrus? Sequitur enim aperte,ostendit quid sit Tyrus, dicens: Ecce Dominus corrumpetorbem terrarum, et vastabit illum, et nudabitfaciem ejus: disperget eos, qui inhabitant in eo, et eritpopulus sicut sacerdos (Isa. XXIV, 1-6). [Num illiusorbis, cujus negotiatio sancta Domino? et famulussicut Dominus et famula sicut domina.] Et erit emenssicut et vendens: et qui debet, sicut ille cui debetur; etqui foenerat, sicut ille qui foeneratur: quia corruptionecorrumpetur terra, et vastabitur vostatione terra. Osenim Domini locutum est haec. Planxit terra, curvatusest orbis terrae, planxerunt alti terrae. Terra autem facinusadmisit, propter eos, qui inhabitant in ea: quia transierunt legem, et mutaverunt jussa testamentiaeterni. Propterea ergo maledictio comedit terram:quia peccaverunt, qui inhabitant in ea. Propter hocegentes erunt, qui inhabitant terram (Isa. XXIV, 1-6).[Numquid illi [36] gentes esse possunt, quibus in omnibusregnis terrae negotiatio est edere, et bibere, etrepleri, non quodam tempore, sed in signum memoriaein conspectu Domini? Et relinquentur hominespauci. Lugebit vitis, lugebit vinum. Gement omnesquorum jocundatur anima. Cessabit jocunditas tympano,cum cessabit impudicitia et divitiae impiorum.Numquid sanctorum cessabit vox citharae? Confusisunt: non biberunt merum, amarum factum est vinumillis, qui bibunt illud. Deserta est omnis civitas: plaudentomnes ne introeant, ululate divini, ubique cessabitomnis jocunditas terrae, et relinquentur civitates desertae, et domus derelictae peribunt (Ibid., 6-8).] Haecomnia erunt terrae in medio gentium. Si desertaest omnis civitas; quae sunt gentes, in quarum medioista faciant? Etsi aliqua horum videntur imperspicuefieri, tamen omnia spiritualia sunt. Omnemcivitatem desertam spiritualiter mortuam dicit:sed Tyri illius meretricis, non cujus negotiatio sanctatoto orbe. Hierusalem autem relinquentur hominespauci, salvo utique statu eorum, qui perimunt. Paucirelinquentur ex eis, quos spiritualiter mortuos dicit:qui per recordationem vixerunt, quos Ecclesiasticusnon interfecerit: sicut multis in locis legimus. Sedquia propositum nobis implendum est, duobus contentisumus exemplis. Minatur Deus ignem ex igniIsrael, regi Assyriorum, id est, adverso corpori, etdicit ad Syrum vel ad stipulam, post paululum, ignemfuturos. Mittet, inquit, Dominus sabaoth, in tuum honorem,ignominiam: et in claritatem tuam, ignem ardentem:et ardebit Israel lumen, et erit tibi ignis, etsanctificabit illud in flamma ardente (scilicet lumenIsrael), et manducabit quasi fenum, silvam. In illo dieardebunt montes: et per praecipitia fugiunt, quasi quifugit a flamma ardente; et qui remanserint ab illis, numerabuntur,et puer scribet illos (Esa. X, 16-19).Qui remanserint, inquit, ab illis. Non enim potestignis, qui comburit [37] ardere? Qui autem ex combustissuperaverint, ignis efficientur. In Zachariategimus, illos remeare quos Ecclesia non occiderit,quod ad se convertantur: caeteros vero spiritualitercruciatibus interficere. Siquidem stantibus oculoseruat, et carnes tabescere faciat: Habitabit, inquit,in Israel confidens: et haec erit strages, qua caedetDeus populos, quotquot militaverunt adversus Israel.Tabescent carnes eorum stantibus eis sub pedes suos: etoculi eorum fluent a foraminibus suis, et lingua eorumtabescet in ore eorum. Et erit in illa die alienatio magnasuper illos, et apprehendet unusquisque manum proximisui, et implebitur manus ejus, manu proximi ejus (idest, caecus caecum ducens). Et Judaea praeliabitur inHierusalem, et colliget viros omnium populorum, etaurum, et argentum, et vestem, in multitudinem nimis.Et haec erit strages equorum, et mulorum, camelorum, et asinorum, et omnium pecorum, quae sunt in castrisillis secundum stragem istam. Et erit, quicumque relictifuerint ex omnibus gentibus convenientibus superHierusalem, et ascendent quotannis adorare regem DominiDeum omnipotentem, celebrare diem festum scenopegiae(Zach. XVI, 11-16). Elam alienigenarum est.Hic speciali jungit generalem, monstratque bipertitam.Haec dicit Dominus: Confringam Nair arcus, inElam principatus eorum. Et excedit speciem. Superducam,inquit, quatuor ventos, a quatuor cardinibuscoeli, nec erit gens quae illuc non veniat, quae expellatElam. Redit in speciem: Et terrebo illos, coram inimiciseorum, qui quaerunt animas eorum, et superducameos secundum iram indignationis meae, et mittampost eos gladium meum, donec consumat eos. Jungitgenus: Et ponam sedem meam in Elam: et perdaminde regem et potentes. Erit in novissimis diebus inaeternum captivitatem, Elam, dicit Dominus (Jerem. XXV,35-38, sec. LXX; sed juxta. Vulg. XLIX, 35-39).]Numquid credendum est non fuisse gentem, quaenon venerit ad expugnandam Elam, aut illic sedesDomini, cujus captivitatem vertit, nisi Ecclesiasticasit figura? Quae vero species: Sinistrae tantum sunt,ut Sodoma, sicut scriptum est: Audite verbum Domini,principes Sodomorum (Isa. I, 10), et quae vocaturspiritualiter Sodoma et Aegyptus: ubi et Dominuseorum crucifixus est (Apoc. XI, 8). Ex his Sodomisexiet Loth, quod est, discessio, ut reveletur homo peccati(II Thess. II, 3). Babylon civitas adversus Hierusalem:totus mundus est in parte sua, quam inhac Israel. Haec convenientur: Visio, inquit, adversusBabylonem, et dicit adversus orbem terrarumventuros sanctos Dei milites: Tollite vicem et exsultatevicem illis, nolite timere, exhortamini; manusaperite magistratus: quia ecce ego praecipio. Sanctificatisunt et vocati gigantes veniunt iram meam leniregaudentes simul et injuriam facientes. Vox multarumgentium in montibus similis gentium multarum, voxregum et gentium collectarum (Isa. XIII, 1-4, sec. LXX):cum Babylonem gens et rex Medorum everterit. Sequiturenim et dicit, qui sint isti reges, et quaeBabylon. Deus sabaoth praecepit genti bellatrici venirede longinquo, de summo fundamento coeli. Deus etbellatores ejus corruperunt universum orbem terrae.Ululate, proximus est enim dies Domini, et contritio a Deo aderit. Propter hoc omnes manus resolventur,et omnis anima hominis trepidabit, Turbabuntur legatiparturientis, et parietes circumstantes, alius ad aliumexpavescent, et facies eorum sicut flamma commutabuntur.Ecce enim dies Domini insanabilis venit indignationiset irae ponere orbem terrarum desertum, etpeccatores perdere ex eo (Ibid., 4-9). [Diem Domini,ex quo passus est, dicit: ex quo spiritualiter interficiturmundus, interficiente exercitu Dei: dum ejuslumen iniqui non vident, sicut serventur, dicens:Stella enim coeli exterioris et omnia luminaria ejus,lumen dabunt et tenebrescet, et non permanebit lumenejus. Et infligam mortuis terrae mala, et injustis peccata eorum, et perdam injuriam scelestorum, et injuriamsuperborum humiliabo.] Et erunt qui remanserint(id est quos supradicti milites non occiderint),honorati magis quam aurum, quod non tetigit ignem,et homo honoratus erit magis quam lapis ex Saphir:Coelum enim indignabitur, et terra commovebitur afundamentis, propter animationem irae Dei in die, quaaderit indignatio ejus. Jungit speciem: Et erit qui relictusest: quasi capreola fugiens, et sicut ovis errans,et non erit qui colligat, ut homo ad populum suumconvertatur, et venire in tribum suam festinet. Quienim inciderit, superabitur; et si qui collecti sunt, gladiocadent, et filiae eorum, in conspectu eorum cadent,et domus eorum diripient, et uxores eorum habebunt.Ecce, excito vobis Medos, qui non computant pecuniam, neque auro opus est illis (Isa. XIII, 10-17).[Subtiliter inserit genus: eum enim [38] estis, nonopus est auro et argento: nisi Ecclesiasticus, quifruitur spiritualiter vita. Sagittationes juvenum confringent,et filiis vestris non miserebuntur, et super nepotesvestros non parcent oculi eorum

(Ibid., 18).]Omnia spiritualiter, sicut de eadem Babylone, scriptasunt: Felix est, qui obtinebit, et collidet parvulos suosad petram (Psal. CXXXVI, 9). Neque enim regem Medorum,quod obtinuerit adversus Babylonem, dixitfelicem, et non Ecclesiasticos, qui obtinent et colliduntfilios Babylonis ad petram scandali. Obtinetautem, sicut scriptum est: Qui obtinet modo, teneat,donec de medio fiat (II Thess. II, 7). Et post multaspeciei et generis, clausura periochiae aperte omnesostendit esse Babylonem, et eos in terra atque inmontibus suis, id est in Ecclesia perdere. Haec dicitDominus: Ponam Babylonem desertum: ut inhabitentin ea erici, et erit in nihilum, et ponam illud lutivoraginem in perditionem. Haec dicit Dominus sabaoth,dicens: quomodo dixi, sic erit: et quemadmodum cogitavi,sic perseverabit, ut perdam Assyrios in terramea et in montibus meis, et erunt in conculcatione, etauferetur ab eis jugum eorum, et gloria ab humeriseorum auferetur. Haec cogitatio, quam cogita it Dominusin orbem terrae totum, et haec manus alta superomnes gentes orbis terrae. Deus enim sanctus quod cogitavit,quis disperget, et manum illam fortem quisavertet (Isa. XIV, 22-27)]? Quotiescumque autempost excidium minatur ruinae civitatis habitationembestiarum, spiritus immundos dicit habitaturos inhominibus, quos sanctus Spiritus deseruit. Non enimhanc injuriam possunt interfecti habitatores, autruinam sentire. Sermones (inquit Amos) quos viditsuper Hierusalem, et coepit. In tribus impietatibusDamasci et in quatuor non aversabor eam, eo quod secabantservis ferreis in utero habentes (Amos I, 1-3).Et iterum: In tribus impietatibus Idumaeae et in quatuornon aversabor eam, propterea quod persecutusest in gladio fratrem suum (Ibid., 11). Et multas aliascivitates alienigenarum in Ecclesiae figura convenit.Ubicumque aut Idamaeam, Theman, Bosor, Seir nominat,fratres malos significat. Sunt autem possessionesEsau. Serras vero ferreas: homines dicit duroset asperos, qui secant parturientes Ecclesias.Item: omnes gentes quae sub coelo sunt, in civitateDei iram Dei bibere et illic percuti, Jeremias testatur,dicens: Sic dicit Dominus Deus Israel: Accipecalicem vini meri de manu tua, et potabis omnes gentesad quas ego mitto te: et voment et insanient a faciegladii, quem ego mitto in medio illarum. Et accepi calicemde manu Domini, et potavi gentes ad quas misitme Dominus ad ipsas Hierusalem et civitates Judae, etreges ejus, et principes ejus: ut ponerentur in desolatione,et in devastatione, et in sibilatione, et Pharaonemregem Aegypti, et pueros ejus, et polentes ejus,universum populum ejus, et omnes promiscuos ejus, etreges omnes alienigenarum, Ascalonem et Gazam et Accaron, et quae contra faciem Azoti, et Idumaeam etMoabitem, et filios Ammon, et regem Tyri, et regemSidonis, et reges qui trans mare sunt, et

Dedan et Theman et Bosor, et omnem circumtunsam a facie, et omnes promiscuos qui commorantur in deserto, et omnes reges Elam, et omnes reges Persarum, et universos reges a subsolano, qui longe et qui juxta sunt, unumquemque ad fratrem suum, et omnia regna terrae quae super faciem terrae sunt, et dices illis: Haec dicit Dominus omnipotens: Bibite et inebriamini, et vomite, et cadetis et surgetis a facie gladii, quem ego mitto in medium vestrum. Et ad eos qui noluerunt accipere calicem, ita ut bibant, dices: Sic dicit Dominus: Bibentes bibetis, quia in civitate in qua invocatum est nomen meum, super ipsam incipio vexare vos: et vos purgatione non eritis purgati, quia gladium ego invoco super inhabitantes terram (Jerem. XXV, 15-29).] Potabis, inquit, Hierusalem, civitates Juda, et reges ejus et principes ejus. Deinde dicit: Et universa regna terrae, quae super faciem terrae sunt: ut ostenderet, ab speciali Hierusalem transitum fecisse ad generalem, in qua sunt omnes gentes terrae, quas illic Deus percutiet, sicut et interpretatus est, dicens: Quoniam in civitatem in qua invocatum est nomen meum, in ipsa incipio vexare vos, et vos purgatione non eritis purgati. Numquid Jeremias, cum esset in corpore qui de Judaeae carcere numquam, nisi tractus, isset in Aegyptum: perspicue adjecto mero in calice id potum daret omnibus gentibus quae sub coelo sunt, aut nunc per Ecclesiam prophetat? Quod si tunc quoque et nunc in Ecclesia locus est, manifestum est, et omnes gentes, ad quas ille Jeremias loquitur, conveniri in principali eorum parte. Si quid enim summum Sathanas, si quid grave, si quid dextrum in suo corpore habet: coelestibus miscuit, ut bellantium mos est, fortibus fortes opponere. Unde Apostolus dicit, non esse sanctis pugnam adversus humanitatem, sed adversus spiritualia nequitiae in coelestibus (Ephes. VI, 12).

Regula V

De Temporibus.

Temporum quantitas in Scripturis frequenter mistica est tropo synecdoche; aut legitimis numeris, qui multis modis positi sunt, et pro loco intelligendi. Synecdoche vero, aut a parte totum est, aut a toto pars. Hoc tropo, 400 annos servivit Israel in Aegypto. Nam dicit Deus Abrahae: Sciens scies, quia peregrinum erit semen tuum in terra non sua, et dominabuntur eorum et affligent eos annis 400 (Gen. XV, 13). Exodi autem Scriptura dicit: 430 annos fuisse in Aegypto (Exod. XII, 40). An non omni tempore servivit? Quaerendum ergo, exquo tempore: quod invenire facile est. Dicit enimScriptura non serviisse populum, nisi post mortemJoseph, et omnium fratrum ejus, et omnium saeculiillius. Filii autem Israel creverunt et multiplicati sunt,et [39] Cethaei fuerunt et praevaluerunt, multiplicabat autemeos terra. Exsurrexit autem rex alter super Aegyptum,qui ignorabat Joseph, et dixit genti suae: Ecce gens filiorum magna Israel multitudo, et valent supernos. Venite ergo circumveniamus eos (Exod. I, 7-10).Si autem post mortem Joseph coepit servire populus,et 530 annis, ex quibus in Aegypto demoratus est,deducimus 80 annos regni Joseph (regnavit enim a30 annis usque in 110) erunt reliqui servitutis Israel,[40] anni 340, quod Deus dixit 400. Si autem omnetempus peregrinationis suae servivit Israel, plus estquam Deus dixit. Si ex morte Joseph secundumScripturae sanctae fidem, minus est. Quo manifestumest, 100 a toto partem esse. Nam post 300 annos,pars aliorum, 100 anni sunt. Propterea dixit, 400 annos.Si hic in omni summa temporis, ut puta post 9dies est, aut post 9 menses: primus dies mensis 10est, sicut scriptum: In utero matris figuratus sum caro 10 mensium congulatus in sanguine (Sap. VI, 2). Sicutautem in prima parte temporis cujusque tempus est,ita in novissima hora totus dies sit; reliquiae milleannorum, mille anni sunt. Sex dies sunt mundi aetas,id est 6000 annorum. In reliquiis sexti dici, id estmille annorum natus est Dominus, passus et resurrexit.Item reliquae mille annorum dictae sunt milleanni primae resurrectionis. Sicut enim reliquiae sextaeferiae, id est, tres horae, totus dies est, unus ex tribussepulturae Domini: ita reliquiae sexti dici majoris quosurrexit Ecclesia, totus dies est, mille anni. Hocenim tropo, constant tres dies et tres nectes. Noctisautem et diei, 24 horae unum tempus est, nec adjiciunturnoctes diebus, nisi certa ratione. Alias, diessolos decimus, sicut Apostolus dicitur mansisse apudPetrum 15. Numquid opus erat dicere, totidem diebuset noctibus? Sic enim scriptum est: Vespere etmane dies unus (Gen. 1-5). Quod si nox et dies, unumtempus est: novissima hora diei, et diem totum etnoctem transactam retinet. Similiter et novissimahora noctis, totam diem et noctem futuram. Horaenim pars est utriusque temporis. Hora qua sepultusest Dominus, pars est sextae feriae cum sua nocte quaetransierat, et hora noctis, qua surrexit, imminentiisest pars diei. Caeterum, si neque in die praesenti noxest praeteria, neque in nocte praesenti dies crastinus:non die resurrexit Dominus, sed nocte. Quoniam diesab ortu solis est, sicut scriptum est: Luminare majusinitium dici (Ibid., 16). Dominus autem ante solis ortumresurrexit. Nam Marcus dicit: Oriente sole (Matth.XVI, 2), non orto, sed oriente, id est, ad ortumeunte: Lucas autem, diluculo (Luc. XXIV, 1). Sed nede hac locutione ambigeretur, alii Evangelistae apertenoctem fuisse testantur. Nam Matthaeus nocte dicitvenisse mulieres ad monumentum, et vidisse Dominum(Matth. XXVIII, 1). Joannes vero, cum adhuc tenebraeessent (Joan. XX. 1). Si autem Dominus antesolem, id est, ante initium diei resurrexit, nox illa,pars erat illucescentis diei. Quod et competit operibusDei, ut non dies obscuraretur in noctem, sed noxlucescat in diem. Ipsa enim nox illuminatur, et efficiturdies: quod est figura eorum, quae facta erantin Christo. Quoniam Deus qui dixit: De tenebris lumenfulgere in cordibus nostris (II Cos. IV, 6). Qui illuminavittenebras, sicut scriptum est: Tenebrae tuaesicut meridies erunt (Isa. LVIII, 10). Et: Nox transivit,dies autem appropinquavit; sicut in die decenter ambulemus(Rom. XIII, 12). Prius est enim quod carnaleest, deinde quod spirituale. Dies ergo primus et novissimus,a toto pars est. Solus medius plenus fuit, avespera in vesperam, secundum conditionem atquepraeceptum. Sicut Moysi dicit: A vespera in vesperam[41] obscuravi diem sabbatorum (Lev. XXIII, 33). Quidamautem dicunt, ex die computandum: quoniam Dominustres dies et noctes dixit, non tres noctes et dies.Sed hoc non longa ratione destruitur. Si enim ex dieinitium sepulturae, in nocte finis: si autem in die finitaest, a nocte coepit. Nam si dies utrimque concluditur,plus erit unus dies. Dicunt praeterea, non possein die esse noctem praeteritam, nec in nocte diem futurum:separatos tres dies et noctes oportere assignari,computante primum diem, quo crucifixus est:alterum, trium horarum reparatarum, tertium sabbati,erit Domini dies 4. Qui autem hanc circumventionemvitant, consentiunt a nocte quidem computandum:sed noctes a diebus debere separari, dicentes,in 3 horis tenebrarum importunarum primamnoctem, alteram sabbati, tertiam illucescentis Dominicae.Noctes quidem veluti tres sunt, sed dies duo.Primus in tribus horis post tenebras: secundus,sabbati. Non enim qui separatos dies promit, potestdicere in nocte qua resurrexit, fuisse diem futurum.Quod si id consentiat, consentiat necesse est, in reliquisdiei sextae feriae, fuisse noctem praeteritam.Quae si tenebrae importunae fuerunt, tres tamen horaelucis, ejusdem sunt diei: nec amiserunt ordinem,quominus pars essent diei ac noctis suae. Tacco 3horas tenebrarum noctem esse non potuisse, quodpraeter ordinem fuerint conditionis Dei. Quidquidenim signi est, non turbat elementorum rationabilemcursum. Non enim quia stetit sol et luna diebusJosue (Jos. X, 13) et Ezechiae (IV Reg. XX, 10), solussol reversus est: aliquid cursus inter solem etlunam mutilatum est et detractum, vel additum dieiaut nocti, et nova exinde coepit temporum aut neomeniaesupputatio, quam statuit Deus in solem et lunam,esse in temporum dies et annos, sicut in

Genesiscriptum est (Gen. I, 17). Multo magis in illodie, nihil turbatum est, cui non sunt adjectae 3 horaetenebrarum, ut essent 15. Namque si solem obscuratum,et rursum ostensum diem dicimus, quod nomen,quem ordinem damus ipsi diei, qui fuisse dicitur,inter sextam feriam et sabbatum, nisi his sabbatumfuit et hebdomada illa 8 dies habuit? Certe,si contentio ratione minime sedari potest, compendioprobamus, 3 horas tenebrarum non pertinere adsepulturam Domini, eo quod adhuc viveret. Nonenim potuit esse in corde terrae, nisi ex quo mortuusvel sepultus est, quod factum est in tribus horissextae feriae, intra duodecimam. Quoniam post occasumsolis, non licebat Judaeis sepelire: cum essetpura coena initium sabbati sicut Joannes dicit (Joan.XIII, 2; XIX, 42). Illic ergo, propter coenam puramJudaeorum, quoniam proximum fuerat monumentumposuerunt Jesum. Dies autem noctibus dignitate,non novitatis ordine praeferuntur; ut omnes masculiprimogeniti sunt, sicut dictum est: Genuit filios etfilias, et obiit (Gen. V). Quod contra legem naturae fit,ut omnes illi masculos primum genuissent. Nobisautem totum tempus, dies est. Omnia nova sunt,figurae transierunt. Ex legitimis numeris sunt, septenarius,denarius, duodenarius. Idem est autem numerus,et cum multiplicatur: ut septuaginta, velseptingenti, vel toties in se: ut septies septem, autdecies deni. Sed aut perfectionem significant, aut aparte totum, aut simplicem summam. Perfectionem,ut septem spiritus. Ecclesiae septem (Apoc. I, 4-11).Aut ut dicit: Septies in die landabo te (Psal. CXVIII,164): aut septies tantum recipiet in isto saeculo (Matth.XXII; Eccl. XXXV, 13). Similiter, denarius, ut aliusEvangelista dicit: Centies tantum recipiet in isto saeculo(Marc. X, 30). Et Daniel, angelorum et coeli velEcclesiae innumerabilem multitudinem denario numerocomplexus est, dicens: Mille millia apparebant illi, et decies millies denaria circumsistebant (Dan. VII,10), Et David: Currus, inquit, Dei decies millies tantum(Psal. LXVII, 18) Et de omni tempore, David:in mille saecula (Psal. CIV, 8). Item, per duodenariumde omni Ecclesia dictum est [42] 14400 et duodecimtribus (Apoc. VII, 4, 5), omnes gentes, sicut:Judicabilis duodecim tribus Israel (Matth. XIX, 28). Aparte totum: quoniam [43] centum tempus legitimisnumeris difinitur, ut in Apocalypsi: Habebitis pressuram10 dies (Apoc. IV, 10); cum significet usque infinem. Septuaginta antem in Babylone, idem tempusesse, importunum est nunc probare. Praeter legitimosetiam numeros, quodcumque tempus in quocumquenumero frequenter breviavit scriptura, sicutsupradictum tempus, Hora appellatum est, dicenteApostolo: Novissima hora est (I Joan. II, 18). Et dies:sicut, Ecce, nunc dies [44] salutationis (II Cor. VI, 2).Et annum praedicare: sicut per Isaiam:

Praedicare annum Domino acceptabilem (Isa. LVI, 2). Quoniam non ille, quo Dominus praedicavit, solus fuit acceptabilis: sed et iste quo praedicat, sicut dictum est: Tempore accepto exaudivi te (Isa. XLIX, 8); et Apostolus interpretatur: Ecce nunc tempus acceptabile (II Cor. VI, 2). Finis denique hujus anni, id est, judicii junxit, dicens: Praedicare annum Domini acceptabilem, et diem retributionis. Et David: Benedices, inquit, coronam anni benignitatis tuae (Psal. LXIV, 12). Aliquando hora, dies et menses, annus est, sicut in Apocalypsi: Parati in horam, et diem, et mensem, et annum (Apoc. IX, 15), quod est, tres anni et dimidium. Ibidem, menses pro annis: Datum est ei delere homines, menses quinque (Ibid., 5). Aliquando, dies denario numero 100 dies sunt, sicut in Apocalypsi: Dies mille ducenti sexaginta (Apoc. XI, 3); nam millies ducenties sexagies centeni centum vigenti sex millia dies sunt, qui sunt anni trecenti quinquaginta, mensibus tricenorum dierum. Ibidem: unus mensis denario numero, 100 menses, ut: Civitatem sanctam calcabunt mensibus quadraginta duobus (Ibid., 2). Nam quadragies bis centeni, 4200 menses sunt, qui sunt anni trecenti quinquaginta. Tempus, aut annus est, aut 100 anni: sicut tempus, et tempora, et dimidium temporis (Dan. VII, 25; XII, 7), quod est, aut 3 anni et dimidius, aut 350. Item: Unus dies aliquando centum annis sunt; sicut de Ecclesia scriptum est: Jacere in civitate, ubi et Dominus ejus crucifixus est, et post tres dies et dimidium (Apoc. XI, 8, 11). Et oportet filium hominis Hierusalem ire, et multa pati a senioribus et principibus sacerdotum, et scribis, et occidi, et post tres dies resurgere (Matth. XX, 18; Marc. X, 33; Luc. XVIII, 32). Ipse enim tertio die resurrexit. Generatio aliquoties et centum anni sunt: sicut Dominus dicit Abrahae: Quarta autem generatione revertetur huc (Gen. XV, 16). In Exodo vero, non de servitutis, sed de totius peregrinationis tempore dictum est: Quinta autem generatione, ascendit populus ex Aegypto (Exod. XII, 42), id est, post 430 annos. Item generatio, aliquoties 10 anni sunt: sicut Jeremias dicit: Eritis in Babylonia, usque ad generationes septem (Baruch. VI, 2). Ternarium numerum, eumdem esse, qui et denarius, idem plenius in Evangelio deprehenditur. Matthaeus enim dicit: tribus servis creditam Domini substantiam (Matth. XXV, 13). Lucas vero decem (Luc. XIX, 13): quos decem in tres redigit, dum et ipse a tribus dicit exactem rationem. Aliquoties unus dies mille anni sunt: sicut scriptum est: Qua die gustaveritis ex arbore, morte moriemini (Gen. II, 17). Et septem dies primi, 7000 anni sunt. Sex diebus operatus est Deus, et requievit ab omnibus operibus suis die septimo, et benedixit et sanctificavit illum (Ibid., 2, 3). Dominus autem dicit: Pater meus usque modo operatur (Joan. V, 17). Sic utenim istum mundum sex diebus operatus est: ita mundum spiritualem, qui est Ecclesia, per 6000 annos operatur, cessaturus die septimo quem benedixit, fecitque in aeternum. Id est quod Dominus inter caetera mandata nihil aliud crebrius praecepit quam observemus et diligamus diem sabbatorum. Qui autem praecepta Dei facit, sabbatum Dei diligat: id est, septimum diem quietis aeternae. Propterea Deus hortatur populum non intrare portas Hierusalem cum onere in die sabbati, et minatur portis, et intrantibus per eas et exeuntibus, sicut Hieremiae mandat, dicens: Vade, ista in portis filiorum populi tui, in quas ingrediuntur reges Juda et egrediuntur, et in omnibus portis Hierusalem, et dices ad eos: Audite verbum Domini, qui intratis portas istas. Haec dicit Dominus: Custodite animas vestras, et nolite tollere onera in die sabbatorum, et nolite exire portas Hierusalem, et nolite ferre onera de domibus vestris in die sabbatorum, sicut mandavi patribus vestris: et non obaudierunt in auribus suis, et induraverunt cervicem suam super patres suos, ut me non audirent, neque perciperent disciplinam. Eritque si me audieritis, dicit Dominus, ut non inferatis onera per portas civitatis hujus in die sabbatorum, ut non facialis omne opus vestrum, et sanctificetis diem sabbatorum, et intrabunt per portas civitatis hujus reges et principes, sedentes in sede David. Et ascendentes in currus et equos, ipsi principes eorum viri Juda, qui inhabitant Hierusalem. Et habitabitur civitas haec in aeternum, et venient de civitatibus Juda, et de civitatibus Hierusalem, et de terra Benjamin, et de terra campestri, et de terra quae ad austrum, afferentes holocausta et incensa, et manna, et thus, ferentes laudationem in domo Domini. Et si me non audieritis, ut sanctificetis diem sabbatorum, ut non portetis onera, neque intretis per portas Hierusalem: succendam ignem in portis ejus, et consumet domos Hierusalem, et non extinguetur (Jerem. XVII, 19-27). Sufficeret breviter mandasse non operari sabbatis. Ut quid: Nolite inferre onera per portas Hierusalem? Aut, si opus erat: et operis speciem diceret, id est, nolite inferre per portas. Non enim aliqui per muros et tecta inferebant onera in civitatem. Hierusalem bipertita est, et portae ejus bipertitae. Per portas inferorum exitur de Hierusalem sancta: et per easdem intratur in maledicta. Qui autem intrant per portas, intrant in aeternam. Hierusalem, ut reges in curribus, et in equis, sedentes in sede David, sicut per Isaiam: Adducent filii filiorum ex omnibus gentibus donum Deo cum equis et curribus [45] in splendore multorum, cum umbraculis in sanctam civitatem (Isa. LVI, 20). Portae sanctae civitatis Jerusalem, Christus est, et vicarii ejus, custodes legis: interficientes vero prophetas et lapidantes ad se missos. Porta diabolus est, et vicarius ejus pseudoapostoli praevaricatores legis, claves regni coelorum alto sensu abscondentes. Ipsi sunt portae, quae non vincunt Ecclesiam, quae supra petram fundata est. Quoniam fundamentum Dei stat, sicut scriptum est: Cognovit Deus, qui sunt ejus (II Tim. II, 19). Si quis autem per praecepta praesidentium cathedrae Moysi introiit, per Christum intrat. Ipsius enim sunt praecepta, ipse exponit onus peccatorum suorum, et sine illo non intrat in requiem sabbati. Si quis vero non per praecepta, sed per facta praesidentium cathedrae Moysi intrat, filius est gehennae magis quam ipsi. Et requiescentibus universis, qui ante sabbatum manna collegerunt: ille cum onere suo inveniatur in die sabbati, in quo non est, manna colligere, neque onus exponere. Quia nolunt audire vocem filii Dei clamantis in Ecclesia et dicentis: Venite ad me omnes qui laboratis et oneriati estis, et ego vos requiescere faciam (Matth. XI, 28). Isti sunt fures, qui non per januam veram, sed per portas suas intrant in suam Hierusalem. Et succendet Deus ignem in portis Hierusalem, et comburet itinera ejus, et non exstinguetur. Ignis enim qui specialis Hierusalem portas exussit, exstinctus est. Apostolus autem sabbatum, et alia legis mandata, figuram esse futuri, sic ait: Nemo ergo judicet vos in cibo et potu aut in parte dici festi, aut neomeniae, aut sabbatorum: quod est umbra futuri (Coloss. II, 16). Multis in locis, unius temporis diversi eventus in speciem separatim describi duo tempora fecerunt, quasi ex ordine se insequentia. In genere autem, uno tempore et uterque eventus: Si 14 anni sub Joseph, ubertatis et sterilitatis 7 anni sunt tantum (Gen. XLI), id est omne tempus passionis Domini, in cujus figura factus est Joseph dominus Aegypti, cum esset 30 annorum. Qui sunt itaque nobis 7 anni ubertatis et saturitatis: idem caeteri 7 sterilitatis et famis. Isto enim tempore minatur Dominus divitibus famem, pauperibus vero saturitatem. Promittit haec bona; et mala duplicis temporis uno tempore futura. Testatur scriptura Exodi (Exod. X), quia manifestum est, omnium plagarum Aegypti immune esse Israel: et per tres dies tenebrarum lumen habuisse. Quod nunc spiritualiter geritur, sicut Deus eidem Pharaoni postea comminatus est dicens: Dabo tenebras super terram tuam (Ibid. 2). Aliquoties unum tempus in multas dividit partes: quarum singulae totum tempus sint. Sic annus quo fuit Noe in arca, dividitur in omnes numeros. Quoties tamen temporum mentio est, quaternarius numerum specialiter tempus est a Domini passione usque in finem. Quaternarius est autem, quoties aut plenus est, aut post tertium pars quarti, ut 340 aut tres et dimidio. Caeteri vero (nam pro locis intelligendi sunt), signa sunt, non manifestae definitiones. Quadraginta ergo diluvii dies totum tempus est. Nam isti sunt 40 anni in Aegypto, et 40 anni in eremo, et 40 dies jejunii Domini et Moysi et [46] Ecclesiae, quibus in Ecclesia jejunat Ecclesia, id est, abstinet a mortuorum voluptatibus. Idem 40 dies quibusmanducat et bibit Ecclesia cum Domino post resurrectionem40 anni sunt quibus erat Ecclesiamanducans et bibens sub Salomone, pace undiqueversum profunda, premente tamen eos bipertitoSalomone: sicut eadem Ecclesia dicit: Pater unusoppressit nos (III Reg. XII, 30). Quadraginta dies, fuitaqua in statu suo, et totidem defecit: ut bis et defectioaquae 10 mense, id est perfecto tempore compleretur.Sed in genere, non ita est, ut quodam temporeinvalescat, et deinde deficiat. Quoniam temporequo valescit carnaliter, eodem deficit spiritualiter,ut ipsa elatio sit defectio, usque dum perficiaturtempus. Sic mundus regnans ponitur sub pedibusEcclesiae filii hominis. Qui sunt itaque 40 dies, exsolvitpeccata Juda, et Israel 149, quod est unumatque idem. Et 7 mense sedit Arca, idem tempus:Et deficiebat aqua usque in 10 mensem, idem tempus.Exivit de arca 12 mense (Gen. VII, 14). Hic estannus libertatis Domini acceptabilis. Quo completo,manifestabitur Ecclesia, mundi pertransisse diluvium.Unaquaeque pars hujus anni, idem annus est.Quale si diceret, exiit de Arca quadragesimo die,aut mense 7 aut 10.

Regula VI

De Recapitulatione.

Recapitulationes sunt istae partes ab initio usquein finem: sicut Adam usque Enoch, id est, Ecclesiaetranslationem, septem generationes, quod est, omnetempus. Rursus ab Adam usque ad Noe, id est,reparationem, decem generationes, quod est omnetempus: et a Noe usque ad Abraham decem generationes.Nam et centum anni, quibus ab Arca fabricataest, omne tempus est quo Ecclesia fabricatur,et eo tempore, in diluvio pereuntibus universis,gubernatur. Quod prudentibus plenius investigandumdata via relinquimus. Quoniam ne copia Scripturaeinterpretando foret; singula persequenda, etea quae hunc intellectum forte impediunt, removendanon putavimus, alio properantes. Inter regulas quibusspiritus lege signavit: quo luminis via custodiretur,nonnihil custodit recapitulatione sigillum ea subtilitate,ut continuatio magis narrationis, quam recapitulatiovideatur. Aliquoties enim sic recapitulat:Tunc illa hora, illo die, eo tempore; sicut Dominusloquitur in Evangelio, dicens: Die qua exivit Loth aSodomis, pluit ignem de coelo, et perdidit omnes(Gen. XIX, 24). Secundum haec, erunt dies filii hominis(Matth. XXIV, 37), quando revelabitur illa ora,qui erit in tecto, et vasa ejus in domo, non descendattollere ea, et qui in agro similiter non revertatur retro(Matth. XIII, 15, 16). Meminerit uxoris Lot (Luc.XVII, 32). Numquid illa hora, qua Dominus revelatusfuerit adventu suo, non debet quis converti adea, quae sua sunt, et uxoris Lot meminisse, et nonantequam reveletur? Dominus autem illa hora, quarevelatus fuerit, jussit ista observari: non solum utabscondendo quaerentibus gratiorem faceret veritatem;sed etiam, ut totum illud tempus, diem velhoram esse monstraret. Eadem itaque hora, id est,tempore, ista observanda mandavit: sed antequamreveletur. Eadem quidem hora: sed in qua partehorae, ratione agnoscitur. Aliquoties autem non suntrecapitulationes hujusmodi, sed futurae similitudines,sicut Dominus dicit: Cum videritis, quod dictumest per Danielem prophetam, tunc qui in Judaeasunt, fugient in montes (Matth. XXIV, 15; Dan. IX, 27).Et inducit finem. Quod autem Daniel dixit: In Africageritur neque eodem tempore finis. Sed quoniamlicet non in eo tamen titulo futurum est. Proptereatunc dixit, id est, cum similiter factum fuerit per orbem:quod est discessio et revelatio hominis peccati.Hoc genere locutionis dicit Spiritus in Psalmis.Cum converterit Dominus captivitatem Sion: facti sumusvelut consolati: Tunc repletum est gaudio os nostrum,et lingua nostra exsultatione. Tunc dicent intergentes, magnificavit Dominus facere cum illis. MagnificavitDominus facere nobiscum: facti sumus laetantes(Psal. CXXV, 1-3). Dicendo vero: Cum averterit Dominuscaptivitatem Sion: tunc dixerunt [47] in gentibus.Nunc avertet, inquit. Tunc dicent in gentibus. Nosenim gentes, quorum captivitatem avertit. Sicut illorumin figuram, tempus habemus dicentes: MagnificavitDominus facere cum eis, magnificavit Dominusfacere nobiscum. De similitudine itaque tempussuum et nostrum, unum fecit et junxit, dicens: Tuncdicent in gentibus, id est, cum similiter gentibus fecerit.Nec illud praetereundum puto, quod spiritus sinemysteriis vel allegoria aliud intelligi voluit. SuperJoannem multi Pseudoprophetae prodierunt in huncmundum. In isto cognoscite spiritus Dei. Omnis spiritusqui solvit Jesum, et negat in carne venisse, deDeo non est, sed hic de Antichristo est. Quod audistisquoniam venit, et nunc in isto mundo praesens est(I Joan. IV, 3). Numquid omnis qui non negat Jesumin carne venisse, Spiritum Dei habet? Sed hanc negationem,in opere non in voce esse, et unumquemquenon ex professione, sed ex fructibus intelligidebere: in omni Epistola qua non nisi de fructibusbonis et malis scripsit, subtiliter admonet, eodemgenere locutionis, sicut dicit: In isto cognoscimuseum, si praecepta ejus custodiamus (I Joan. II, 3, 4).Qui autem dicit: Quoniam cognovi eum et mandataejus non servat, mendax est. Numquid ex professionedixit intelligi fratrem qui Deum nescit, et non exoperibus? Et qui dixerit, quoniam diligit Deum, etfratrem suum odit: mendox est (1 Joan. IV, 20). Sienim ut dicit, diligit Deum: doceat operibus, adhaereatDeo, diligat Deum in fratre. Si credit Christumincarnatum; quiescat odire membra Christi. Si creditVerbum carnem factum: quid persequitur incarne, Verbum caro factum (Joan. I, 14). Quid persequiturverbum in carne? Quod dixit Dominus:Quamdiu fecistis uni ex fratribus meis minimis in me credentibus, mihi fecistis (Matth. XXV, 40): non opereturmalum in Christi carne, id est, in servis ejus,quoniam Dominus et Ecclesia, una caro est. In quacarne si credit esse hominem: cur non diligit, autquod crudelius est, cur odit, sicut scriptum est:Qui non diligit fratrem, permanet in morte (I Joan. III,14). Et, qui fratrem suum odit, homicida est (Ibid.,14). Aliud majus evidentius signum cognoscendiAntichristi non esse dixit, quam qui negat in carne,idem odit fratrem? Tale autem quod dicit: Quoniamqui negaverit Christum in carne, de Deo non est(II Joan. XVII): quale, Nemo potest dicere DominusJesus, nisi in Spiritu sancto (I Cor. XII, 3): cummulti dicant Dominum Jesum, ipso contestante:Non omnes qui mihi dicunt, Domine, Domine, introibunt in regnum coelorum (Matth. VII, 21). Sed hocloco Apostolus, neminem posse dicere Dominum JesumChristum, nisi in Spiritu sancto secundum conscientiamdixit (I Cor. XII, 3), secundum interioremhominem, non secundum solam professionem, utostenderet illis, qui dicunt Dominum JESUM, nihilminus habere ab his, qui charismatum generibusextolluntur. Sed unum atque eumdem Spiritumpossidere omnem, qui Dominum Jesum crediderit,idem operibus credidisse monstraverit. Nemo, inquit,potest dicere Dominum Jesum, nisi in Spiritusancto: Divisiones autem sunt charismatum, idem verospiritus. Et divisiones ministeriorum sunt: et idemDominus (Ibid., 4, 5). Solvere autem Jesum, est nonfacere quod Jesum fecisse confitetur, sicut idem Dominusdicit: Qui solverit unum ex mandatis istis minimis,et sic docuerit homines, minimus vocabitur inregno coelorum (Matth. V, 20). Et quid sit solverit, exconsequentibus aperit, dicens: Qui autem fecerit, etsic docuerit. Hanc ergo negationem, operum esse,non vocis, et Paulus apostolus confirmat dicens:Dominum scire confitentur, factis autem negant (Tit. I,16). Et iterum: habentes formam pietatis, virtutemautem ejus negantes (II Tim. III, 5). Hoc sensu dicitquosdam fratres, Christum non voce sancte praedicare,sed corde. Nam voce sancte praedicant. Consentitdenique praedicationi eorum, et mandat audiri,dicens: Quid interest sive per occasionem, siveper veritatem Christus annuntietur (Philipp. I, 18).Dominum enim Christum Antichristus non voto, sedoccasione praedicat. Alio tendens, per Christi nomeningreditur: quo sibi viam sternat, quo sub Christinomine, ventri pareat, et his (quod turpe est dicere),sanctitatis et simplicitatis nomen imponat, signis etprodigiis cubiculorum opera Christum esse asseverans.Quos salubri cautione vitare admonet Apostolusdicens: Filiis abstinete vos a simulacris (I Joan. V, 21).

Regula VII

De diabolo et corpore ejus.

Loci duo illustrati, Isaiae cap. XIV, Et Ezech. XXVIII.De diabolo et corpore ejus breviter videri potest,si id quod de Domino et ejus corpore dictum est,id quoque observetur. Transitus namque a capite adcorpus, eadem ratione dignoscitur, sicut per Isaiamde rege Babylonis dicitur: Quomodo cecidit Lucifer decoelo, mane oriens? contritus est in terra qui mittebaturad omnes gentes? Tu autem dixisti in animo tuo:In coelum ascendam, super stellas Dei ponam sedemmeam, sedebo in monte alto super montes altos in aquilonem,ascendam super nubes, ero similis Altissimo.Nunc autem ad inferos descendisti in fundamenta terrae.et qui viderint te, mirabuntur super te, et dicent: hicest homo, qui concitat terram, movet reges, qui ponitorbem terrae totum desertum. Civitas autem destruxitabductosque non solvit. Omnes reges gentium dormierantin honore, in domo sua. Tu autem projectus es inmontes velut mortuus, abominatus cum omnibus qui cecideruntin desertis gladio, et descenderunt ad inferos.Quomodo venisti: sicut vestimentum sanguine conspersum non erit mundum, ita nec tu eris mundus,quia terram meam perdidisti, et plebem meam occidisti.Non eris in aeternum tempus semen nequam, para,filios tuos interfice, peccatum patris tui non resurgant(Isai. XIX, 12, 22). In regem Babylonis, et omnesreges, et omnis populus significatus, unum enim estcorpus. Quomodo, inquit, cecidit de coelo lucifer,mane oriens, confractus in terra: qui mittitur ad omnesgentes? Tu autem dixisti in animo tuo: In coelumascendam, super stellas Dei ponam sedem meam. Diabolushoc sibi promittit. Non enim sperat retinendoin coelum posse ascendere, qui ne dejiceretur, resisterenon valuit. Multo magis ista homo sperare nonpotest: et tamen hominem esse sic dicit: Hic esthomo qui incitat terram. Sed praeter hanc rationem,quam neque diabolus, neque homo sperare potest,se posse in coelum ascendere, et super stellas Deisedens, similem se Deo fieri, etiam ipsa Scripturaaliud inquirendum admonet. Nam si in coelum et suprastellas Dei dicit se sedem suam positurum: quomodoin monte alto sedebit, aut super montes inaquilonem vel in nubibus ut similis sit Altissimo?non enim Altissimus in hujusmodi habet sedem.Coelum, Ecclesiam dicit: sicut procedente Scripturavidebimus. De hoc coelo cadit lucifer matutinus.Lucifer enim bipertitus est: sicut Dominus dicit inApocalypsi de se et de suo corpore: Ego sum radixet genus David, et stella splendida matutina, sponsuset sponsa (Apoc. XXII, 16). Item illic: Qui vicerit, daboilli stellam matutinam (Apoc. II, 28): id est, ut sitstella matutina sicut Christus, quem accepimus.Pars ergo lucifer, id est, adversum corpus, quod estdiabolus, reges, et populus, cadit de coelo, et confringiturin terra. His regulis dicit Sapientia: Auditeergo reges et intelligite: discite judices finium terrae,praebete aures, qui continetis multitudinem, et placetisvobis in turbis nationum: quoniam data est vobispotestas a Domino, et virtus ab Altissimo; qui interrogabitopera vestra, et cogitationes scrutabitur.Quoniam, cum essetis ministri regni illius, non rectejudicastis, neque custodistis legem (Sap. VI, 2, 3).Rex ergo Babylonis totum corpus est: sed pro locisintelligimus, in quam partem corporis conveniat.Cecidit de coelo lucifer, in omne corpus potest convenire.In coelum ascendam, super stellas Dei ponamsedem meam, similiter, et caput: majores, qui stellarumDei, id est, sanctorum dominum dominandumputant, cum ipsorum minores dominentur,sicut scriptum est: Major serviet minori (Gen. XXV,25). Huic Esau, id est, fratribus malis, sic dicitDominus per Abdiam prophetam: Exaltans habitationemsuam, dicens in corde suo: Quis me deducetad terras? Si exaltatus fueris sicut aquila, et interstellas ponas nidum tuum, inde te detraham, dicit Dominus(Abd. I, 3, 4). Sedebo in monte alto super montesaltos, in aquilonem, ascendam super nubes, erosimilis Altissimo (Isa. XIV, 13). Mons altus, populusest superbus. Montes alti, singuli quique, qui adunatimontem faciunt, id est, corpus diaboli. Multosenim esse montes malos, dicit Scriptura: Transferenturmontes in corde maris (Psal. XLV, 3). Iterum:Fundamenta montium conturbata sunt, et commota sunt,quoniam iratus est Deus (Psal. XVII, 8). Nam et corpusDomini, id est, Ecclesia, mons dicitur: et singuli quiEcclesia, faciunt montes, sicut scriptum est: Ego autemconstitutus sum rex ab eo, super Sion montem sanctumejus, annuntians imperia ejus (Psal. II, 6). Et iterum:Perdam Assyrios in terra mea, et in montibus meis (Isa.XIV, 25). Et iterum: Suscipiant montes pacem populo,et colles justitiam (Psal. LXXI, 3). Et iterum: Montesexsultabunt velut arietes, et colles velut agni ovium(Psal. CXIII, 4). Deus in monte Sion habet sedem,et in montibus Israel, et in nubibus sanctis suis:quod est Ecclesia. Scriptum est:

Timeat a facie Domini omnis terra: quoniam exsurgit de nubibus sanctis (Psal. XXXII, 8). Iterum, nubibus mandabo, ne pluant super eam imbrem (Isa. V, 6). Iterum: Nimbus et nubes in circuitu ejus (Psal. XCVI, 2). Et quod in monte Sion habitet, sic dicit: Cognoscetis, quia ego sum Dominus Deus vester, habitans in Sion monte sancto meo (Ezech. XXXV, 3). Et diabolus in monte sedet, sed Seir, qui est Esau, id est, fratrum malorum: quem montem Deus increpat per Ezechielem, et dicit in laetitia universae terrae desolaturum, quod adversum Israel inimicitias exerceat. Ipse est mons, ipsi montes Aquilonis. In his diabolus sedet; et nubium coeli veluti dominatur. Hactenus, se similem dicit altissimo (Isa. XIV, 14). Duae sunt partes in Ecclesia, Austri et Aquilonis, id est, Meridiana et Septentrionalis. In parte meridiana, Dominus manet. Scriptum est: Ubi pascis, ubi manes in meridiano (Cant. I, 6)? Diabolus vero, in Aquilonem, sicut Deus dicit populo suo: Illum persequar ab Aquilone a vobis, et expellam illum in terra sine aqua, id est, in suos; et exterminabo faciem ejus in mare primum, et posteriora ejus in mare novissimum, quod est in populos primos et novissimos (Joel. XI, 10). Instar Ecclesiae, fabricatus est iste mundus, in quo Sol oriens, non nisi per Austrum, id est, meridianum iter habet; et decursa Australi parte, invisibilis vadit in locum suum rediens. Sic et Dominus Deus noster Jesus Christus, Sol aeternus partem suam percurrit, unde et meridianum vocat. Aquiloni vero, id est, adversae parti non oritur: sicut iidem cum in judicium venerint, dicent: Justitiae lumen non luxit nobis (Sap. V, 6). Timentibus autem Dominum, oritur Sol justitiae: et sanitas in pennis ejus, sicut scriptum est (Malach. IV, 2). Malis vero meridie nox est: sicut scriptum est: Dum sustinent ipsi lumen, factae sunt illis tenebrae, fulgorem obscura nocte ambulaverunt, palpabunt sicut caecus parietem, et cui non sunt oculi, palpabunt et cadent meridie, quasi media nocte (Isa. LIX, 9, 10, sec. LXX). Iterum: Occidet sol meridie, et tenebricabit super terra dies luminis (Amos VIII, 9). Iterum: Propterea nox erit vobis de visione, et tenebrae vobis erunt ex divinatione, et occidet sol super prophetas, et obscurabit super eos dies luminis (Mich. III, 6). Huic populo ex Austro comminatur Deus, sicut per Ezechielem Soor increpat, dicens: Spiritus Austri contrivit te (Ezech. XXVII, 16). Is enim confringere permittit, dicens: Exsurge, Aquilo, et veni, Auster: perfla hortum tuum, et defluent unguenta mea (Cant. IV, 16). Exsurgente enim nequam spiritu, resistit Spiritus sanctus, qui Domini hortum perflat, et eliciuntur unguenta, id est, odor suavitatis offertur. Et per Ezechielem, idem ex reliquiis populi mali sic dicit Deus, adducere super populum suum, partem ejusdem populi, quod est mysterium facinoris: Ecce ego super te Gog, principem Mosoch et Tobel: et congregabo te, et adducam te, et ponam tea novissimo Aquilone, et adducam super te montem Israel: et perdam arcum de manu tua sinistra, et sagittas tuas de manu dextera, et dejiciam te super montes Israel (Ezech. XXXIX, 1-4). Hoc autem geritur, a passione Domini: quoadusque de medio ejusdem mysterii facinoris discedat Ecclesia, quae detineat, ut in tempore suo detegatur impietas, sicut dicit Apostolus: Et nunc quid detineat, scitis, ut in suo tempore detegatur: Mysterium enim jam nunc operatur iniquitatis: tantum, ut qui detinens detinet modo, donec de medio fiat. Et tunc revelabitur ille impius (II Thess. II, 6-8). Et in Hieremia legimus, peccatores Israel in Aquilone convenire, Domino dicente: Vade et lege sermones istos ad Aquilonem, et dic: Convertere ad me, domus Israel, dicit Dominus (Jerem. III, 3). Meridianum vero pars est Domini; sicut et in Job scriptum est: A meridiana parte germinabit tibi vita (Job. XI, 17). Aquilo diaboli: Utraque autem pars, in toto mundo. Ascendam, inquit, nubes: ero similis Altissimo. Nunc autem ad inferos descendes in fundamenta terrae. Qui viderint te, mirabuntur super te, et dicent: Hic est homo qui concitat terram, commovet reges, qui ponit orbem terrae totum desertum. Numquid in diabolum convenit, Qui viderint te, mirabuntur super te? Aut in regem novissimum, cum ad inferos descendes? Ipso enim ad inferos descendente, non erit qui miretur, mundo finito. Non enim dicent: Hic est homo qui concitavit terram, reges, et posuit orbem terrae totum desertum: sed incitat, et commovet et ponit. Hominem enim totum corpus dicit tam in regibus quam in populis: cujus hominis superbi partem cum Deus percutit, et ad inferos dejicit, dicimus: Hic est homo qui incitat terram, commovet reges, scilicet sanctos: Qui ponit orbem terrae totum desertum: irridentium vox est, non confirmantium, sicut ibi: Qui dissolvit templum, et triduo illud suscitat (Marc. XV, 29). Dixit enim: Fortitudinem faciam, et sapientiam intellectus. Auferam terminos nationum, et fortitudinem illarum vastabo, et comminuam civitates cum habitantibus: et totum orbem comprehendam manu, velut nidum, et velut ova derelicta auferam, et non erit qui effugiat me, aut contradicat mihi (Isa. X, 13, 14). Numquid ista quae sibi promittit, valet implere? Ponit quidem orbem terrae totum desertum, sed orbem suum. Civitates autem destruxit, utique sui orbis. Est enim bipertitus, mobilis et immobilis: sicut Paralipomenon: Commoveatur a facie Domini omnis terra. Etenim fundavit orbem terrae, qui non commovebitur. Abductosque non solvit (I Par. XVI, 30; Ps. XCV, 9). Potest, inquit, in speciem convenire; quod captivis in nullo relaxasset, sed inimicis raptum aestimans, principali tota in eos uteretur potestate. Quod objurgat Deus, dicens: Ego quidemiratus sum modice: ipsi autem adjecerunt in mala(Zach. I, 15). Verumtamen in figuram generalitatisfacta et dicta sunt, et spiritualiter implentur: dumhi qui dominantur, humilitatis subditos aut tentationiscausa vel merito sibi subditos sine respectupietatis atque communis conditionis affligunt, quibusnon sufficit potestas, sed ea immoderatius uticontemnunt, quod culpat, dicens: Persequentes retributionem(Isai. I, 23). Et iterum: Extendit manumsuam ei in retribuendo (Ps. LIV, 21). Parum est enimquod inimicus est; adhuc gestit et in subditumvindicare, sicut scriptum est: Omnes subditos vobiscompungitis. Dissimulans odisse Dominum, inimicumet vindicatorem: quod per vindictam quamsoli sibi Deus exceptavit, aliquid sanctitatis usurpet.Scriptum est enim: Mihi vindictam, et ego retribuam,dicit Dominus (Rom. XII, 19). Omnes reges terrae dormieruntin honore, homo in domo sua (Isai. XIV, 18,19). Reges, sanctos dixit. Nam non omnes reges velprivati in domo sua dormierunt, sicut sancti indomo (sua) quam delegerunt. Tu autem projectus esin montes velut mortuus abominatus, cum omnibus quiceciderunt inserti gladio, et descendunt ad inferos.Diabolo dicit, Projectus es in montes, in quibus sedet.Denique non dixit mortuus: sed velut mortuusabominatus. Adhuc enim vivit: licet ipse in suis gladioperimatur, et ad inferos descendat. Sicut enimDominus, quidquid sui patiuntur, se pati dixit(Matth. XXV, 40): ita et diabolus ipse in suis inculcatur,ipse abominatus confringitur, sicut scriptumest: In diminutione populi, comminutio principis(Prov. XIV, 28). Diabolus ab homine suo non separatur:nec homo in quo diabolus non est, potest dicere:Ero similis Altissimo. Nec diabolus, hic homo,qui incitat terram: nisi in homine fuerit. Sicut Dominus,homo dici non potest, nisi in homine; nechomo, nisi in Christo. Sed quid in quem conveniat,pro locis observandum est. Iterum corpus ipsiusdiaboli convenit dicens: Quomodo venisti? sicut vestimentumsanguine conspersum non est mundum, itanec tu eris mundus: quia terram meam perdidisti, etplebem meam occidisti. Non eris in aeternum tempus,semen nequam: para, filios tuos interfice peccatis patristui, ut non resurgant (Isai. XIV, 19-21, sec. LXX). Hicostendit non convenire in speciem. Rex enim Babylonis,qui terram Domini vastavit, et populum occidit,id est, Nabuchodonosor mundus obiit, in aeternumvivit: corpori dicit sui cujusque temporis pararequos genuerit, interfici peccatis ejus quo ipse, quiconvenitur genitus. Novissimus enim rex non filios,sed fratres habere potest. Neque velut mortuus cumad inferos descenderit, sed mortuus. Per Ezechielemsic Deus increpat regem Tyri: Quoniam exaltatumest cor tuum, et dixisti: Deus ego sum, habitationeDei habitavi in ordine maris. Tu autem homo es, et non Deus: et dedisti cor tuum tamquamcor Dei. Numquid sapientior es tu Daniele? Sapientesarguerunt te sapientia tua. Numquid sapientiatua aut doctrina tua fecisti tibi virtutem et aurumet argentum thesauris tuis? Numquid in multa doctrinatua, et in mercatu tuo multiplicasti virtutemtuam? Propterea haec dicit Dominus: Quoniam dedisticor tuum, sicut cor Dei: propter hoc, ecce ego inducosuper te alienas pestes ex gentibus, et exinanientgladios tuos super te, et super decorem doctrinae tuae:et vulnerabunt decorem tuum in perditionem, et deponentte, et morieris morte vulneratorum in corde maris.Numquid dicturus es in conspectu interficientium te:Deus ego sum? Tu vero homo es, et non Deus. In multitudinemincircumcisorum peribis, in manibus alienorum: quia ego locutus sum, dicit Dominus. Tu es signaculummultitudinis et corona decoris: in deliciis paradisiDei fuisti, omnem lapidem optimum habens in tealligatum; Sardium, Topazum, Smaragdum et Carbunculumet Sapphirum, et Jaspin, et argentum etaurum et Ligyrium et Achatim et Ame histum, Chrysolithumet Beryllum, et Onychium: et auro replestithesauros tuos et apothechas tuas. Cum Cherubin posuite in monte sancto Dei: fuisti in medio lapidumigneorum, abiisti sine macula in diebus tuis, ex qua diecreatus es, donec invenirentur iniquitates tuae in te. Amultitudine negotiationis tuae implesti promptuaria tuainiquitate et peccatis: et vulneratus es a monte Dei.Abduxit te Cherubin de medio lapidum inferorum, exaltatumest cor tuum in corde tuo: corrupta est doctrina cum decore tuo. Propter multitudinem peccatorum etiniquitatem negotiationis tuae, contaminata sunt sanctatua: educam ignem de medio tui, hic te devorabit. Etdabo te cinerem in terra tua, in conspectu omnium videntiumte, et omnes qui te noverunt inter nationes,constristabuntur super te. Perditio factus es, et non erisin aeternum tempus (Ezech. XXVIII, 2-19, sec. LXX).[Quoniam exaltatum est, inquit cor tuum, et dixisti:Deus ego sum, habitatione Dei habitavi in corde maris:et in hominem convenit dicentem: Ego sum Christus;et in diabolo qui in corde maris, id est, populihabitat, sicut Deus in corde sanctorum suorum sedet.Populus, in corde maris, id est, in voluptate velaltitudine saeculi habitat, sicut in alio loco dicit Deuseidem civitati: Satiata et honorata es nimis in cordemaris. In [48] qua multa deduxerunt te remiges tui: SpiritusAustri contrivit te in corde maris virtutis tuae.]Tu autem homo es, et non Deus (Ezech. XXVII, 25-26).Et diabolus in homine, homo dictus est: sicut Dominusdixit in Evangelio: Inimicus homo hoc fecit(Matth. XIII, 28). Et interpretatus est, dicens: Quiea seminat, diabolus est (Ibid., 39). Homo diaboli,Deus esse non potest. Propterea in utrumque convenit:Tu homo es, et non Deus. Dedisti cor tuum,tamquam cor Dei. Numquid sapientior es tu Daniele?In Daniele, totum corpus est Ecclesiae: quia nonpotest esse peccati sapientior in negotiis vitae, sicutille sapientior est in suo quam filii lucis. Potest etiamin speciem convenire: quoniam Daniel specialiterconfundit regem Babylonis, in figuram, qui Propheticospiritu regem superbum ad confessionem uniusDei, Ecclesiastica majestate prostravit; qui confessionesuarum virtutum, et coelesti sapientia, Babylonissuperstitiones evertit. Sapientes te [49] non argueruntsapientia tua. Non solum enim Daniel sapiens,sed etiam tres pueri, qui regem et omne regnumejus cum ipsis diis suis, unum Dominum asserendo,eodem Deo praesente confuderunt. Iidem nunc usquegeneraliter ejusdem tam externas quas intestinasBabylonis, lumine veritatis disrumpunt. Numquid inscientia tua, aut sapientia tua fecisti tibi virtutem, et aurum et argentum thesauris tuis? Numquid inmulta scientia, aut in mercatu tuo multiplicasti tibivirtutem tuam? et exaltatum est cor tuum in virtutetua. Putant enim superbi et beneficiorum omnipotentisDei ingrati, sua virtute aliquid posse, et sapientiaditari, nescientes scriptum esse: Non levibus cursus,non fortibus praelium, neque sapienti panis(Eccl. IX, 11). Et iterum: Numquid magnificabitursecuris sine concisore (Isa. X, 15)? Et non quidemprudentibus divitiae, et non scientibus gratia. Haecenim non sunt in nostra potestate, sed a Deo conferuntur.Quid enim habes, quod non accepisti? Si autemaccepisti, quid gloriaris, tamquam non acceperis(I Cor. IV, 7)? Et iterum: Non glorietur sapiens,in sapientia sua (Jerem. IX, 23). Propterea haec dicit Dominus: Quoniam dedisti cor tuum, sicut cor Dei:Propterea, ecce ego induco super te alienos, pestes exgentibus: et exinanient gladios suos super te, et superdecorem scientiae tuae. (Ezech. XXVIII, 7, 8). Etsi potestin speciem convenire, quod reges saeculi persuam superbiam, dominos se appellari patiuntur;tamen hoc quoque convenit in genus. Frequenterenim inducit Deus in Ecclesiam alienigenas, etmultos in morte vulnerat. Sed etiam occulta persecutionemultos inducit ex gentibus, in quibustentet populum suum, et occidat nequam per similes,sic Matthatiam. Et vulnerabunt decorem tuum in perditionem. Aliquos enim non in perditionem,sed cum spe sanitatis vulnerant. Et deponent te, idest, humiliabunt: et morieris morte vulneratorumin corde maris. Non diceret vulnerato, morierismorte vulneratorum: nisi quia non aperte vulneratur,et moritur: sed ipse est, in quibus vulneratur.Numquid narrans narrabis in conspectu inter ficientiumte: Deus sum ego? Id est, numquid divini generistitulis terrebis eos, quibus traditus fueris, tam spiritualiterquam carnaliter? Tu vero homo et non Deus,in multitudine incircumcisorum periturus es manibusalienorum: quia ego locutus, dicit Dominus. Nunc aperuit,quo genere se ille dicat Deum: dum minaturet in multitudine incircumcisorum periturum manibusalienorum: quod non convenit, nisi in eum quisibi circumcisus videtur. Rex enim Tyri, mortemsolam potuit timere: Nonne a circumcisis, aut cumeis moreretur. Et factus est sermo Domini ad me,dicens: Fili hominis accipe lamentum super principemTyri, et dic illi: Haec dicit Dominus: Tu es signaculumsimilitudinis, et corona decoris in paradiso Deifuisti. Numquid diabolo factus es paradisus, ut ipsequod paradisum perdiderit, increpetur? Homo fuitin deliciis paradisi, ipse est signaculum similitudinis,qui ad similitudinem Dei factus est. Signaculum autemad decorem dixit: sicut per Aggaeum dimicantibushujus adversum se fratribus promittit Deus Ecclesiae,dicens: Ego commovebo coelum et terram,mare et aridam; et convertam currus et sessores. Etdescendent equi et sessores eorum unusquisque in gladio ad fratrem suum. In die illo dicit Dominus omnipotens,accipiam te Zorobabel filium Salathiel, servummeum, et ponam te signaculum, quoniam te elegi, dicit Dominusomnipotens. Zorobabel, omne corpus est (AggaeiII, 22-24; Eccl. XLIX, 13). Etenim exinde nusquamlegimus commotum supra se venisse Zorobabel. Hicest ex tribu Juda, qui sub Dario meruit aedificareHierusalem. Ipse quoque in figura fundavit domumDei, et perfecit sicut idem Dominus dicit: ManusZorobabel fundaverunt domum hanc, et manus ejusperficient eam (Zach. IV, 9.) Quod est autem signaculumhoc et corona speciei, sicut Deus promittitEcclesiae dicens: Videbunt gentes justitiam tuam, etreges claritatem tuam, et vocabunt nomen tuum, quodDominus nominavit. Illud erit corona speciei in manu Domini, et diadema regni in manu Dei tui. Tu etiamnon vocaberis derelicta: et terra tua non vocabitur deserta.Tibi etiam nomen vocabitur, voluntas mea, etterra tua orbis terrarum (Isa. LXII, 2-4.) Homo estitaque signaculum similitudinis, et corona speciei:cujus pars, in ipso decore divinae similitudinis, etdeliciis paradisi, id est, Ecclesiae perseverat. Alteravero pars, ne in aeternum vivat, inter ipsam atquearborem vitae, flammeus ensis evolvitur (Gen. III,24). Adam namque, sicut Apostolus dicit, umbra futuriest (Rom, V, 14). Sic et hi fratres, divisus est inCain et Abel. Omnem lapidem optimum habens in te alligatum; Sardium, et Topazium, et Smaragdum, etCarbunculum, et Sapphirum, et Jaspin, argentum etaurum, et Liguriam et Achaten et Amethistum et Chrysolitumet Beryllum et Onychium: et auro replestithesauros tuos, et apothecas tuas in te. Haec et indiabolum conveniunt, et in hominem. Isti enimduodecim lapides et aurum et argentum, omnesquethesauri diabolo adhaerent delegati. Denique, habesin te alligatum: Et iterum: Apothecas tuas in te.Sicut corpus Domini a sanctis ornatur: promittenteDeo et dicente: Extolle oculos tuos in circuitu; videomnes filios tuos, collecti sunt, et venerunt ad te. Vivoego, dicit Dominus, quia omnibus illis indueris, et superimponesillos: sicut ornamentum novae nuptae, quiadeserta tua et diruta, et quae ceciderunt, nunc angustiabuntur ab inhabitantibus (Isa. XLIX, 18, 19; LX,14). Et in Apocalypsi, eadem civitas duodecim lapidibusfundata construitur (Apoc. XXI, 19, 20). Omnia,inquit, lapidem optimum, et enumeravit duodecim:ut ostenderet in duodenario numero perfectionem.Omnia, enim, quae fecit Deus, bona sunt (Gen. I, 25).Horum diabolus usum, non naturam mutavit. Etomnes homines excellenti sensu et potentis ingenii,aurum sunt et argentum, et lapides pretiosi secundumnaturam: sed ejus erunt in cujus obsequio,natura, suis fruuntur. Quoniam, cui se signaveritquis in obedientia: servus est ejus, cui obaudit, sivepeccati, sive justitiae. Ita fit, ut et diabolus habeataurum et argentum, et lapides pretiosos. Omniaquidem, non sua secundum originem: sed sua, secundumvoluntatem. Nam et in Job scriptum estdiabolo: Omne aurum maris sub eo est (Job. XLI, 21).Et Apostolus, vasa aurea et argentea, dicit esse quaedamin contumeliam (II Tim. II, 20). Non enim, sicutquidam putant, omnia lignea et fictilia reprobavit,cum ex eis sint aliqua in honorem, ipso dicente:Figulum luti, aliud quidem fingere in honorem, aliudvero in contumeliam (Rom. IX, 21). Et ex ligno,aliud ad praeparationem esse, aliud in sacrilegium:ex auro et argento, id est, ex magnis et perspicuisdixit immundos. Nam et in Apocalypsi: Meretrix(id est, corpus adversum) purpura, cocco, et auro,et argento, lapidibusque pretiosis ornatur: habens poculumaureum in manu, plenum exsecrationum et immunditiarumtotius terrae (Apoc. XVII, 4). Ista suntergo diaboli ornamenta, lapides pretiosi: quibuslapides igneos imitatur, et homo in se habet thesaurostam facinorum quam perspicuos. Ipse enim suorumportator est, quem facultates suae velut compedesligaverunt. Praeter illa, quae ab utroque sexucorporis diaboli ornanda eduntur: etiam his, quaedefossa habent, insitum est cor. Ubi enim erit thesaurus,illic erit et cor hominis (Matth. VI, 21). Vetusenim homo et terra ejus, unum corpus est: quoniamipse quoque terra est. Unde Apostolus non solumea, quae corpore admitti possunt, sed et avaritiam,membrum esse possidentis, ita definivit dicens:Mortificate itaque membra vestra, quae in terra sunt,fornicationem, immunditiam, passionem, concupiscentiam malam, et avaritiam, quae est idolorum servitus.Propter quae venit ira Dei (Coloss. III, 5, 6). Ex quadie creatus es tu cum Cherubim, imposui te in montesancto Dei (Ezech. XXVIII,

14), id est in Christo, vel Ecclesia. In medio lapidum igneorum fuisti, id est hominum sanctorum, qui adunati, montem Dei faciunt. Angeli enim alterius substantiae, lapides dici non possunt, quia corpus non habent. Abiisti sine macula tu, in diebus tuis: ex qua die creatus es tu, donec invenirentur iniquitates tuae in te, a multitudine negotiationis tuae (Ibid., 15). Lapides, Ecclesiam esse sic dicit Petrus: Ecce vos fratres, tamquam lapides vivi, coaedificamini in domos spirituales (I Pet. II, 5). Quam domum, igneam esse; et hanc, malos fratres ardere sic dicit Deus: Erit domus Jacob, ignis: domus autem Joseph, flamma: Domus vero Esau, stipula. Exardescent in illos et comedent eos: et non erit ignifer in domo Esau, quoniam Dominus locutus est (Abd., 18). Cum enim peccat homo dejicitur de monte Dei, et non erit ignifer, amisso Spiritu, et succendetur in cinerem. Peccasti, et vulneratus es a monte Dei: et abduxit te Cherubim de medio lapidum igneorum. [Cherubim, ministerium Dei est: quod exclusit universos malos de Ecclesia, sed spiritualiter. Qui enim vestimentum nuptiale non habet, hic in saeculo excluditur de medio recumbentium. Denique in tenebras, id est, in obdurationem mittitur; donec in ignem in aeternum descendat. Futuro enim saeculo, nemo miscebitur choro sanctorum, qui postea excludatur. Exaltatum est cor tuum in decore tuo, corrupta est scientia tua in decore tuo.] Corrupta est scientia ejus, qui sciens prudensque erat et studio affectatae sapientiae asserit dissimulata veritate, mendacium: sicut Spiritus dicit: Cum cognovissent Dominum, non ut Dominum magnificaverunt, aut gratias egerunt: sed nugati sunt in cogitationibus suis, dicentes esse sapientes (Rom. I, 22). [Corrupta est scientia eorum, qui alios docent, se ipsos non docent. Corruptus est decor, qui generi suo operum similitudine non respondet. Propter multitudinem peccatorum tuorum. In terram projeci te: In conspectu regum dedi te dehonestari (Ezech. XXVIII, 18). Et diabolus est in terram, id est, in hominem, et homo de sublimitate Ecclesiae, in conculcationem, si Hieremias dicit: Dejeci de coelo in terram gloriam. In conspectu regum (Thren. II, 1). Christianorum dixit: quorum pedibus conculcatur diabolus et homo ejus; Propter multitudinem peccatorum tuorum, et iniquitatem negotiationis tuae, contaminantur sancta tua.] Videtur veluti principalem titulum exprobrasse, corpore diaboli, negotiationis magis dicit, et thesauros, spirituales nequitiae. Sicut enim spiritualis justitiae negotiatio, est thesaurus, ut dicit Dominus: Simile est regnum coelorum homini negotiatori (Matth. XIII, 45). Et iterum: Thesaurizate vobis thesauros in coelo (Matth. VI, 20). Iterum: Dedit servis suis substantiam suam, ut negotiarentur (Luc. XIX, 13). Iterum:

NegotiatoresCarthaginenses resistentib. etc. (Ezech. XXVII, 12).Iterum: Negotiatio ejus et merces sancta Domino(Isac. XXIII, 18). Et Apostolus: Est, inquit, negotiatiomagna, pietas (I Tim. VI, 6). Ita spiritualis nequitia,negotiatio est thesaurus peccatorum, sicut Dominusdicit: Homo malus, de thesauro cordis emittitmala (Matth. XII, 35.) Et Apostolus: Thesaurizastibi iram in die irae (Rom. II, 5).Propter iniquitatem, inquit, negotiationis tuae contaminantursancta tua. Qui enim non recte sanctitateDei utitur, suam efficit, sicut Deus dicit de sabbatissuis: Sabbata vestra odit anima mea. Educam ignemde medio tui: hic te devorabit (Isa. I, 13). Ignis, Ecclesiaest: quae cum discesserit e medio mysteriifacinoris, tunc pluet ignem Dominus a Domino, deEcclesia, sicut scriptum est: Sol exortus est super terram,et Lot intravit in Segor: et pluit Dominus super Sodomam et Gomorrham, sulphur et ignem a Dominode coelo (Gen. XIX, 23). Hic est ignis, quem supradixit: Domus Jacob, ignis: domus autem Esau, stipula.Exardescent in eos, et comedent illos: et nonerit ignifer in domo Esau (Abd., 18). In Genesi iterumscriptum est: Cum contereret Deus omnes civitates in circuitu, commemoratus est Deus Abrahae, et emisit Lote medio subversionis: cum subverteret Deus civitates,in quibus inhabitabat in eis Lot (Gen. XIX, 29.) NumquidLot non merebatur propria justitia liberari, utdiceret Scriptura: Commemoratus est Deus Abrahae,et emisit Lot e medio subversionis? Aut, In civitatibushabitabat, et non in civitate: ut diceret, Civitates, inquibus habitabat? Sed prophetia est futurae discessionis.Memor enim Deus promissionis ad Abraham,ejecit Lot de omnibus civitatibus Sodomorum, quibusveniet ignis ex igni Ecclesiae, quae de medioeorum educetur. Et dabo te in cinerem in terra tua,(Ezech. XXVIII, 18.) Id est, in hominibus vel ipsoshomines in terra sua, qui in terra Dei esse noluerunt.In conspectu hominum videntium te, id est, intelligentium.Numquid diabolus in homine videripotest? Et omnes, qui te noverunt inter nationes, contristabuntursuper te (Ibid., 19.) Cum enim Dominuspercutit aut detegit malos, constristantur qui eorumauxilio fulciri solent, corporis sui parte debilitataPerditio facta es: et non eris in aeternum.Has Regulas Tichonii expendit Augustinus tom. III, lib. III de Doctr. Christ. capp. 30-37.

The Scriptorium Project is the work of a small group of lay people of various apostolic churches who are interested in the preservation, transmission, and translation of the works of the early and medieval church. Our efforts are to make the works of the church fathers accessible to anyone who might have an interest in Christian antiquities and the theological, philosophical, and moral writings that have become the bedrock of Western Civilization.

To-date, our releases have pulled from the Greek, Syriac, Georgian, Latin, Celtic, Ethiopian, and Coptic traditions of Christianity, and have been pulled from sundry local traditions and languages.

SEVEN RULES

www.ingramcontent.com/pod-product-compliance
Lightning Source LLC
LaVergne TN
LVHW012046070526
838201LV00079B/3636